it needs
P (5),

IMAGES
of America

CAPE COD
CANAL

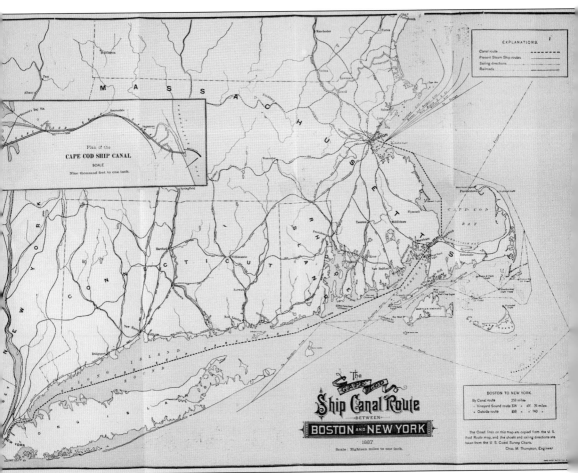

This 1887 map, drawn up for Frederick A. Lockwood's Cape Cod Ship Canal Company, illustrates a proposed route between Boston and New York that would be shorter and safer than traveling around Cape Cod. The inset shows its path across the neck of the cape, past the train station at Buzzards Bay and the riverside villages of Bourne, Bournedale, and Sagamore. Although Lockwood's efforts were not successful, they set the general path that the Cape Cod Canal would take two decades later. (Map by Charles M. Thompson.)

ON THE COVER: A workman rows out to the dredge *Governor Warfield* as its shovel scoops up another load of mud in the final stretch of the canal in 1914. The *Governor Warfield* is working toward its sister dredge, the *Governor Herrick* (just out of the frame to the left), as both cut through the final blockade, Foley's Dyke. (Courtesy Historic New England.)

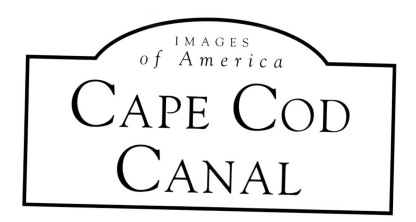

IMAGES
of America

CAPE COD CANAL

Timothy T. Orwig for Historic New England

ARCADIA
PUBLISHING

Copyright © 2013 by Historic New England
ISBN 978-1-4671-2036-4

Published by Arcadia Publishing
Charleston, South Carolina

Printed in the United States of America

Library of Congress Control Number: 2013934391

For all general information, please contact Arcadia Publishing:
Telephone 843-853-2070
Fax 843-853-0044
E-mail sales@arcadiapublishing.com
For customer service and orders:
Toll-Free 1-888-313-2665

Visit us on the Internet at www.arcadiapublishing.com

To all those who worked to build the Cape Cod Canal and to Nina Heald Webber, who sought out and preserved these amazing images.

CONTENTS

ACKNOWLEDGMENTS

Cape Cod Canal is a collaboration between Historic New England, the oldest, largest, and most comprehensive regional heritage organization in the nation, and Arcadia Publishing, the largest publisher of regional history books in North America. Both share a singular dedication to place, to preserving the details of extraordinary events and everyday life, and to making that information easily accessible to a wide audience. Historic New England has been collecting photographic images and ephemera for more than a century; this book is based on one of its most recent acquisitions, a treasure trove of Cape Cod Canal material donated by Nina Heald Webber. Nina Heald Webber has been fascinated by the Cape Cod Canal for years and has sought out images and memorabilia relating to all aspects of its history. In addition to the photographs featured here, her collection includes books, magazines, ephemera, banners, matchbook covers, crate labels, and much else, all testifying to the cultural significance of the Cape Cod Canal.

Unless otherwise noted, all images appear courtesy of Historic New England. Photographers are credited wherever possible. Special thanks are given to those who allowed us publication rights to some of these images, listed as follows: Bourne Historical Society, the Curtis Teich Postcard Archives, and the William Brewster Nickerson Cape Cod History Archives, located at Cape Cod Community College in West Barnstable.

I would like to thank the staff at Historic New England, without whose hard work this volume would not have been possible, and Rebekah Collinsworth, editor at Arcadia Publishing, for her patience and perseverance. Finally, I thank my family, Alan and William, for their love and encouragement in this process.

INTRODUCTION

Cape Cod is the bared and bended arm of Massachusetts: the shoulder is at Buzzard's Bay; the elbow, or crazy-bone, at Cape Mallebarre; the wrist at Truro; and the sandy fist at Provincetown,— behind which the State stands on her guard, with her back to the Green Mountains, and her feet planted on the floor of the ocean, like an athlete protecting her Bay,—boxing with northeast storms, and, ever and anon, heaving up her Atlantic adversary from the lap of earth,—ready to thrust forward her other fist, which keeps guard the while upon her breast at Cape Ann.

–Henry David Thoreau, *Cape Cod* (1865)

Today, most people experience the Cape Cod Canal as part of a brief exhilarating view far below as they zip across the Bourne or Sagamore Bridges, on their way from the mainland of Massachusetts to their Cape Cod vacation. But the centennial of the opening of the Cape Cod Canal in 1914 gives us an opportunity to examine anew the early history of this monumental achievement. The widest sea-level canal in the world, the Cape Cod Canal shortened water travel from Boston to New York by about 70 miles, bypassing some of the stormiest and most treacherous passages of the Atlantic coast. The canal transformed Cape Cod, which Thoreau called "the bared and bended arm" of Massachusetts, from a peninsula into an island. While for many the Cape Cod Canal marks a dividing line between the world of commerce and the world of leisure, the canal retains essential components of each.

The need to find a shortcut across Cape Cod is ancient, as is the route of the canal. Native American travelers avoided the long, treacherous water passage from Cape Cod Bay to Buzzards Bay by crossing the peninsula at its narrowest point. They would paddle up the Scusset or Manomet Rivers and then carry their small boats over the low hills between the two valleys.

Miles Standish, the military leader of the Plymouth Colony, first advocated building a canal here in 1623. William Bradford established the Plymouth Colony's Aptucxet Trading Post along the Manomet (later known as Monument) River in 1627. Because the British navy ruled the waters of the Outer Cape, George Washington had to supply the Continental Army via an overland route through the valley that would become the Cape Cod Canal. In 1776, he authorized the first of many canal surveys.

In the succeeding years, while great canals were built elsewhere, plans for a canal across Cape Cod languished. By the Civil War, railroads brought an end to the great age of canal building in the United States, and a railroad traversed Cape Cod. In 1870, the Cape Cod Ship Canal Company was formed but failed to turn over a shovel until 10 years later; the company ended ignominiously with 400 unpaid Italian laborers roaming the streets of Sandwich begging for food. The company reformed in 1883 and, under Frederick A. Lockwood, worked sporadically, managing to dig a ditch 7,000 feet long in Sandwich.

Every subsequent effort failed until 1909, when August Perry Belmont (1853–1924) began digging. Belmont was the grandson of Commodore Matthew Perry, a man instrumental in the 1854 opening of Japan to the West, and the son of August Belmont, a German financier who rebuilt New York banking after the Panic of 1837 and became chair of the Democratic National Committee. August Perry Belmont was a man of many accomplishments, beginning with his student days at Harvard University, where, as a sprinter, he invented spiked track shoes. An avid fan and supporter of Thoroughbred horse racing, he owned the Kentucky Nursery Stud farm, which produced champion horses such as Man o' War, and built the Belmont Park racetrack on Long Island in 1905. More importantly, the Interborough Rapid Transit Company, which Belmont founded in 1902, opened New York City's first subway line in 1904. To the building of the Cape Cod Canal, Belmont brought the connections, experience, and public relations skills necessary to succeed where so many had failed before.

The building of the Cape Cod Canal is one of the 20th century's great stories of engineering and technological achievement. Belmont became interested in the canal in 1904. He asked William Barclay Parsons (1859–1932), the engineer who had worked with him on the New York subway system, to conduct test borings along every mile of the route and to determine if the canal was feasible. Next, Belmont created a new company to secure financing for this gigantic project: the Boston, Cape Cod, and New York Canal Company. Its board of directors and backers were the wealthy elite, whose yachts would join the parade of ships through the canal on its opening day. A second Belmont company, the Cape Cod Construction Company, submitted the successful bid for constructing the canal in 1907. It bought up the remaining land (in addition to the land Frederick A. Lockwood had secured in the 1880s) and in 1909 hired the subcontractors who would do the actual work. Parsons served as chief engineer, overseeing the subcontractors who dug the channel through tidal rivers, marshes, and the deep sand of Cape Cod. The work was plagued by chronic equipment failures, occasional flooding, and the sinking of several vessels as well as by unexpected numbers of enormous glacial boulders. The builders had to relocate roadways, houses, railroad lines, depots, and a trolley line. They deepened and widened the bay approaches and river channels and cut several miles of new channels between the rivers. Finally, they had to build new breakwaters, bridges, and wharves.

The Cape Cod Canal changed forever the sleepy farming, fishing, and tourist villages that made up the town of Bourne (Sagamore, Bournedale, Bourne, and Buzzards Bay) and transformed two short tidal rivers into a major national waterway. Where the canal crossed the northwestern corner of Sandwich on its way to Cape Cod Bay, it opened up new wharves for Sandwich's more established factories and commerce. Both towns gained wider recognition, commerce, and tourism.

August Belmont's new canal opened to acclaim in 1914, although it was overshadowed by preparations for war in Europe. The era of the great sea canals began in 1869 with the Suez Canal and concluded in 1914 with the Cape Cod Canal and the Panama Canal. Even after the Cape Cod Canal opened, Belmont continued to work to widen and deepen it, but the tolls were never enough both to pay off construction and turn a profit. In May 1918, after a German submarine attacked a ship on the Outer Cape, Pres. Woodrow Wilson recognized the strategic importance of the Cape Cod Canal and ordered the government to take control of it. After the war, the government negotiated with Belmont and his company for another decade to acquire the canal.

In 1928, Congress finally authorized the purchase of the canal, and the Army Corps of Engineers began a sustained series of improvements to what was now a free public canal. Providing welcome jobs in the Great Depression, the project included three new bridges, which opened in 1935, and a deeper channel by 1940. While the canal has remained an engineering marvel and a vital shipping link, its role as a center of leisure came to the fore in these years. Beloved by boaters and a summer destination for a century, the Cape Cod Canal continues to be a national treasure.

One

AMBITION

SANDWICH, BOURNE, AND
LOCKWOOD'S DITCH

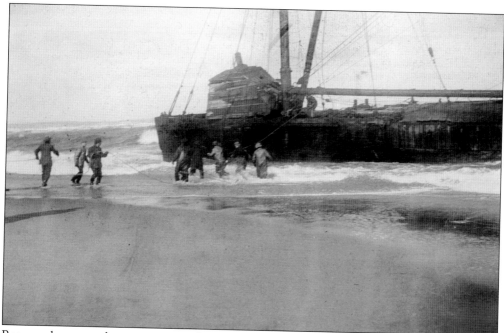

Rescuers brave rough seas to secure a line to an unknown shipwreck in this image from an early glass-plate negative. More than 5,400 shipwrecks litter the shores of Maine, New Hampshire, Massachusetts, and Rhode Island. Half of these wrecks were around Cape Cod, ranging from the little *Sparrowhawk* in 1626 to the luxury liner *Andrea Doria* in 1956, with new wrecks each year.

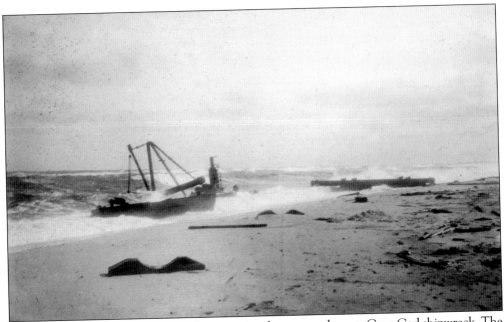

Another image from an early glass-plate negative shows an unknown Cape Cod shipwreck. The same storms that tear apart ships also uncover centuries-old wrecks; in 1863, the *Sparrowhawk* reemerged and was partially salvaged, more than 200 years after it had sunk. The pirate ship *Whydah*, which sank off Wellfleet in 1717, taking all but 2 of her crew of 146, has been salvaged by deep-sea divers. Some wrecks in shallower waters are protected for recreational diving.

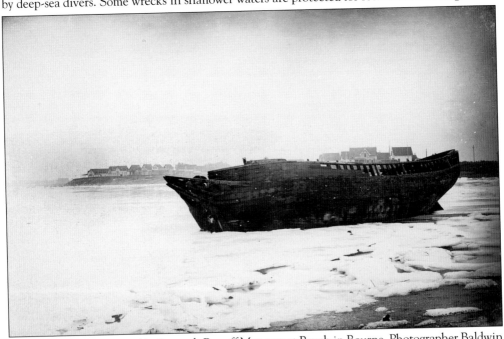

The *Splendid* went aground in Buzzards Bay off Monument Beach in Bourne. Photographer Baldwin Coolidge (1845–1928), great-grandson of Loammi Baldwin (builder of the Middlesex Canal in Massachusetts), recorded the wreck in 1918. Coolidge gave up a career as an engineer to become a commercial photographer; he especially loved Cape Cod. (Photograph by Baldwin Coolidge.)

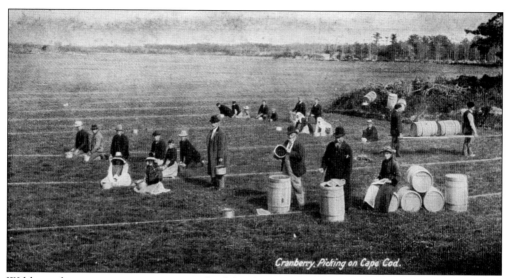

Wild cranberries were an important food for the Wampanoag and other tribes of the region, and they were long a part of the Thanksgiving tradition. Cranberries were first commercially grown in the early 19th century in Dennis on Cape Cod and continue to be produced on Cape Cod today.

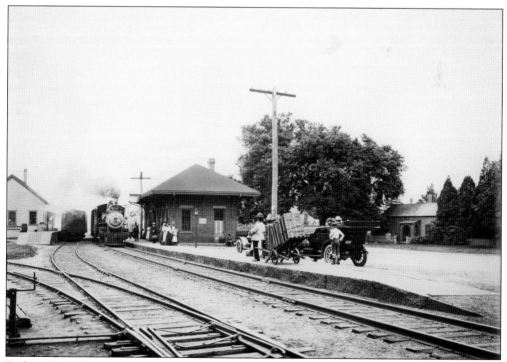

Early in the 20th century, passengers and automobiles line up to wait for the train at the Sandwich train depot. Founded in 1637 and incorporated two years later, Sandwich is the oldest town on Cape Cod. The first trains arrived in 1848, and Sandwich remains the transportation link between most of Cape Cod and the mainland. (Photograph by Thomson and Thomson.)

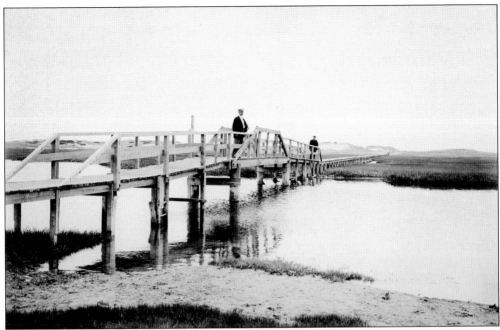

The Cape Cod Canal cuts through the marshy western edge of Sandwich, following the tidal delta of the Scusset River east to Cape Cod Bay. This 1907 image shows the Beach Walk, built over the marshes, and a bridge over one of the tidal river channels, with large sand dunes in the background. (Photograph by New England News.)

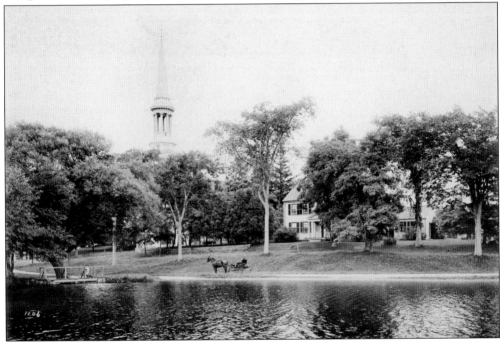

A horse and carriage pause on the path along Shawme Pond in Sandwich Center Village in 1916. The Congregational church (built 1847) and the Dunbar House (1740) are in the background. (Photograph by New England News.)

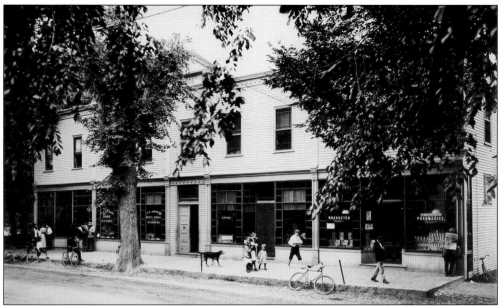

Early in the 1900s, the Novelty Block was home to the Sandwich Post Office, F.F. Jones Shoe Store, A.P. Wing, and W.R. Procter, Pharmacist. (Photograph by Thomson and Thomson.)

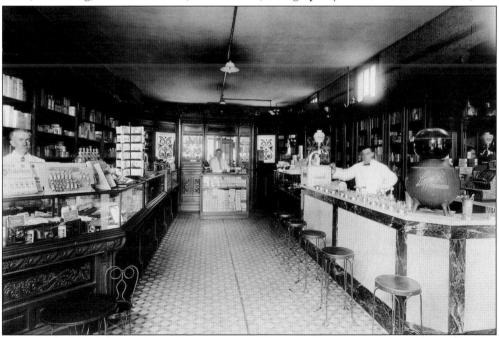

W.R. Proctor's Pharmacy, shown here around 1907, was richly appointed, with carved wooden counters and cabinets and leaded glass mirrors. Three clerks wait for customers behind counters piled high with Harmony Toothpaste, Prince Albert tobacco, and Philip Morris cigarettes. The soda jerk behind the marble-fronted soda fountain is slightly blurred, having moved during the long exposure necessary for the interior photograph. The street outside, as seen in the photograph at the top of this page, is reflected in the globe atop Liggett's Orangeade. (Photograph by New England News.)

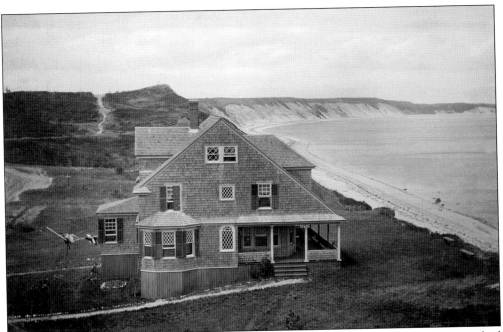

This early postcard shows Sagamore Highlands in Bourne, with a Shingle-style cottage perched high atop bluffs overlooking Cape Cod Bay, just west of the Cape Cod Canal. In 1884, the western half of Sandwich became the independent town of Bourne. The wing wall of the canal lessened the erosion of these cliffs while speeding erosion in Sandwich.

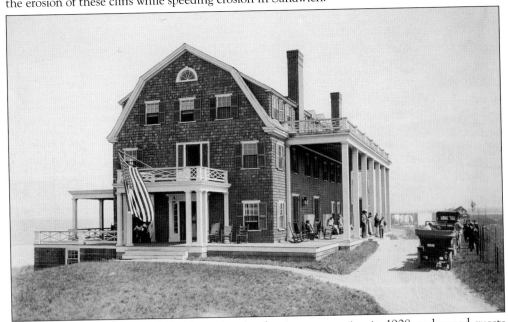

The Bradford Arms Hotel, shown here shortly after its construction in 1908, welcomed guests to Sagamore Beach until 1935, when it burned down. Most of Sagamore was undeveloped until 1905, when members of the nondenominational Christian Endeavor Society (founded 1881) bought numerous lots and built a summer colony. Francis E. Clark, the society's founder, built a summerhouse in Sagamore. (Photograph by Thomson & Thomson.)

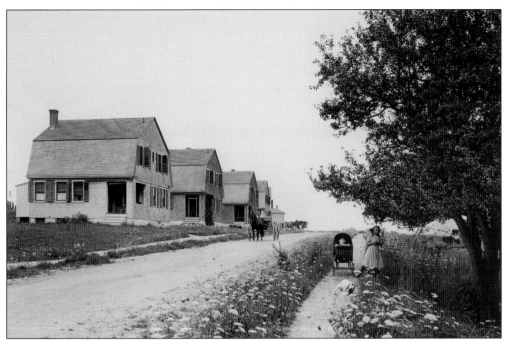

Children play along newly built Savary Avenue in Sagamore about 1908; in that year, Francis E. Clark's Christian Endeavor Society boasted 3.5 million members worldwide. Within a decade, Savary Avenue overlooked the new Cape Cod Canal. (Photograph by Thomson and Thomson.)

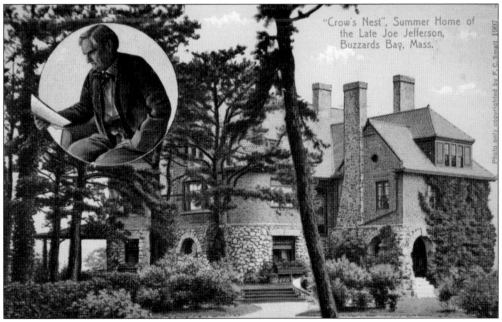

The Crow's Nest was a summer home that actor Joseph Jefferson (1829–1905) built in Bourne. Born into a theater family, Jefferson began acting at age three. He was a natural comedian and was best known for his version (cowritten with Dion Boucicault) of *Rip Van Winkle*, a role he performed in London in 1865 and worldwide for the rest of his life and even committed to film in 1896. (Photograph by Fred C. Small.)

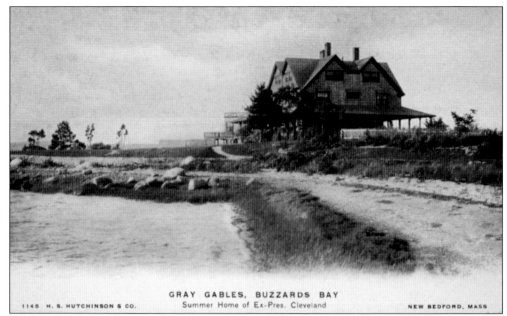

GRAY GABLES, BUZZARDS BAY
Summer Home of Ex-Pres. Cleveland

1145 H. S. HUTCHINSON & CO.   NEW BEDFORD, MASS

Joseph Jefferson convinced his friend Pres. Grover Cleveland to buy a summer home in Bourne. In 1888, Cleveland bought Tudor Haven, which he renamed Gray Gables. Cleveland served two terms as president of the United States, 1885–1889 and 1893–1897. The estate served as the Summer White House intermittently from 1888 to 1896; Navy ships used a special dock. Later known as the Gray Gables Ocean House inn, it burned in 1973. (Published by H.S. Hutchinson and Company.)

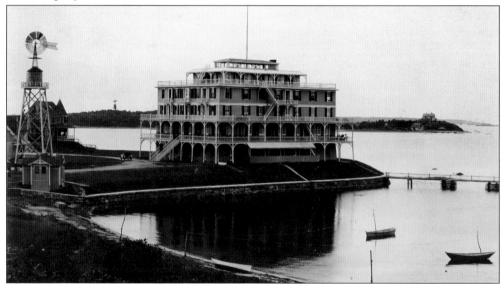

Shown in a photograph from about 1910, Norcross House (c. 1884) was a large summer hotel built by James A. Norcross, one of the famed Norcross Brothers builders who worked with architect H.H. Richardson. It boasted a seawall of red granite rejected from the quarries during the building of Richardson's Allegheny County Courthouse. A landmark both from the shore and to boaters on Buzzards Bay, it advertised in the Boston newspapers that "All rooms overlook the water. Always cool." (Photograph by New England News.)

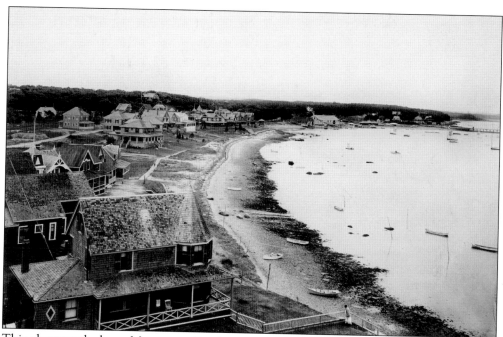

This photograph shows Monument Beach as seen from Norcross House. Monument Beach, a village along Buzzards Bay just south of the future path of the canal, was built up as a summer colony by wealthy families from Brockton and Worcester, Massachusetts. (Photograph by Thomson and Thomson.)

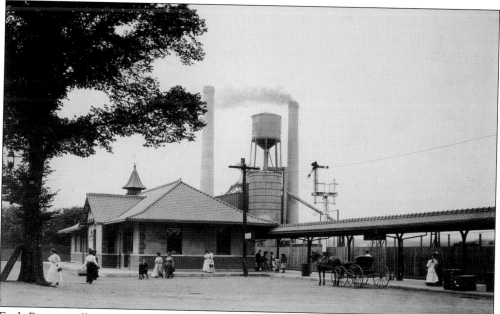

Each Bourne village had its own railway station, including this Sagamore station, built in 1911 to replace the former station demolished for the Cape Cod Canal. Bourne's first station was built in 1848 in what became known as Buzzards Bay. The town began to boom after the Woods Hole Railroad line from Boston opened in 1872, with a stop in Buzzards Bay. (Photograph by Thomson and Thomson.)

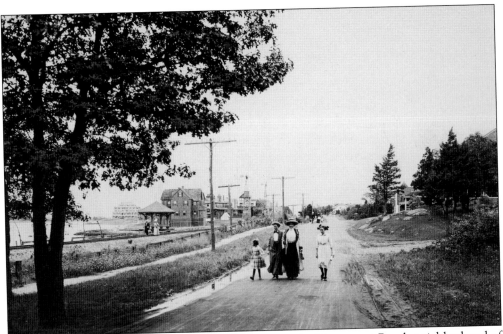

After a rain, vacationers stroll down Tobey Avenue in the Monument Beach neighborhood of Bourne. The Woods Hole Railroad line parallels the road to the left, and Norcross House is visible in the distance on the shore of Buzzards Bay. The Monument Beach railroad station opened in 1875. (Photograph by Thomson and Thomson.)

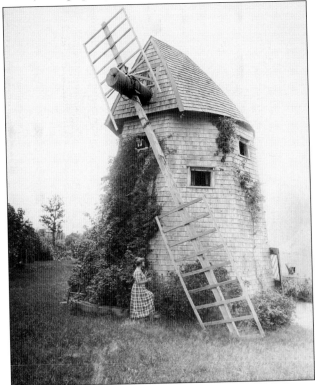

Two young costumed women pose at the Rothery Windmill in Cataumet. The southernmost Bourne village of Cataumet was the site of a summer colony for residents from Brookline, Massachusetts. Antiquarian photographer and journalist Mary H. Northend (1850–1926), author of *Colonial Homes and Their Furnishings* (1912), often staged photographs such as this to promote Colonial Revival sites and ideals, which found a ready market among editors and readers. (Photograph by Mary H. Northend.)

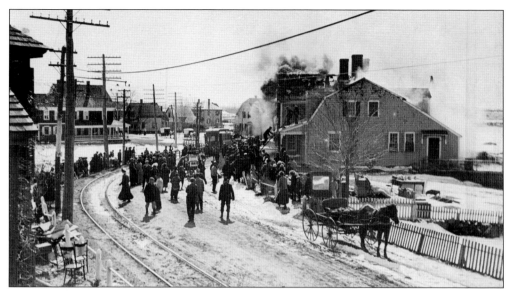

On March 8, 1911, fire destroyed the Old Bourne Home.

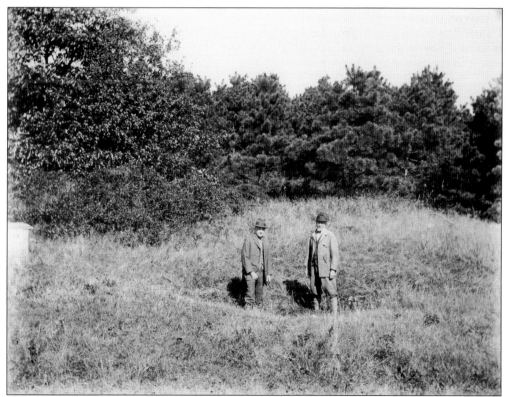

In 1926, Percival Hall Lombard (1872–1932) and Nathan Bourne Hartford (1861–1948) of the Bourne Historical Society excavated this cellar hole near the Cape Cod Canal, looking for the original Aptucxet Trading Post of 1627. They found metalware, slipware, and window glass and were able to mark the site with a tablet in time for the post's tercentenary.

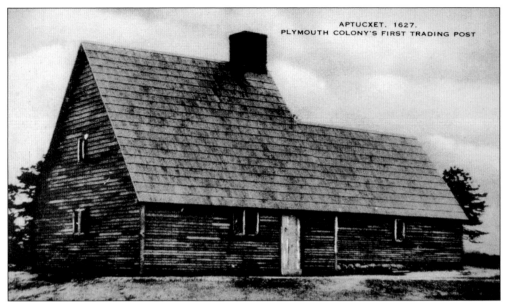

Despite skepticism that greeted his earlier findings, Percival Lombard built a replica of the Aptucxet Trading Post on the foundations he had excavated. He first engaged restoration architect Joseph Everett Chandler to draw up the plans but eventually chose a design by architectural restorer George Francis Dow and his carpenter brother Eugene Dow. Their replica opened in 1930. (Courtesy of Bourne Historical Society.)

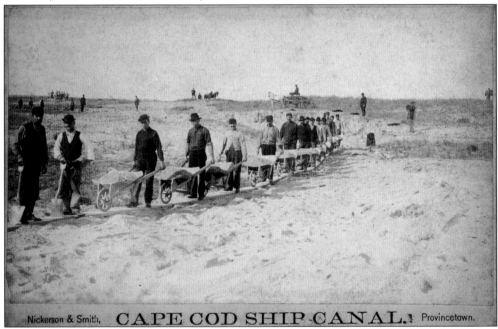

A series of cabinet cards by Provincetown photographers George A. Nickerson and William Smith document the construction that began in 1880 for the Cape Cod Ship Canal. At 7:00 a.m. on September 15, James Keenan dug the first shovelful of dirt. In this shot, two-dozen Italian immigrant workmen are shown lined up with shovels and wheelbarrows as they start digging the canal by hand. (Photograph by Nickerson and Smith.)

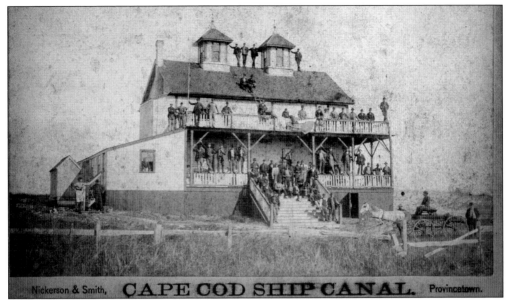

Nickerson & Smith, **CAPE COD SHIP CANAL.** Provincetown.

This cabinet card appears to show the boardinghouse for some of the workers in 1880; most slept in tents. Workmen have obliged the photographer by perching on or hanging from the railings, while others have climbed to the roof, where three of the most adventurous stand arm-in-arm between the roof cupolas. The workers, as many as 500 at the height of the effort, were never paid. After begging for food on the streets of Sandwich, they were shipped by the trainload to New York. (Photograph by Nickerson and Smith.)

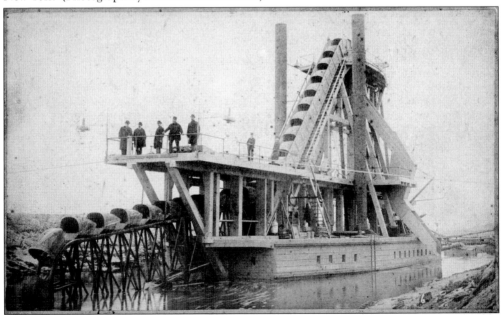

Frederick A. Lockwood, a manufacturer from East Boston who specialized in marine equipment, headed up another effort to build the canal in 1883. Lockwood had the East Coast rights to a newly invented bucket dredge, which he built and towed to the marshes of Sandwich in March 1884. It had a continuous conveyor belt of 39 hopper buckets that scooped up mud, raised it 56 feet in the air, and dumped it into discharge pipes. (Photograph by Nickerson and Smith.)

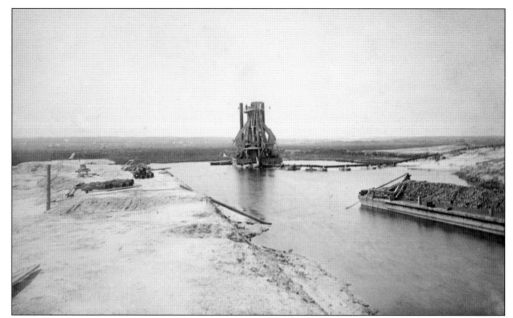

This rare view shows the *Lockwood* at work on the canal in 1884, with its discharge pipe deployed off to the right, toward the west. Though Frederick A. Lockwood made substantial progress, company management and financing collapsed, and Lockwood overextended his credit to keep working. In 1889, Lockwood's East Boston shop burned, and he fell seriously ill. His successors worked sporadically until their charter lapsed in 1891.

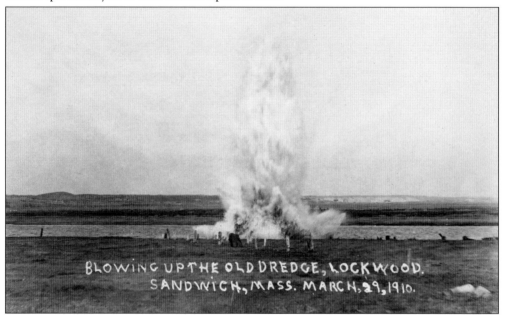

BLOWING UP THE OLD DREDGE, LOCKWOOD.
SANDWICH, MASS. MARCH, 29, 1910.

Stripped of equipment and burned, the dredge *Lockwood* was abandoned in its channel after work ceased in 1891. Two decades later, on March 29, 1910, the hull was blown up to clear the way for the final, successful effort. Although derided as Lockwood's Ditch, this trench, over a mile in length, made up about a tenth of the final canal. Lockwood's company, in fact, had purchased most of the land necessary to complete the canal in 1914.

Two

ENGINEERING
BUILDING THE CANAL

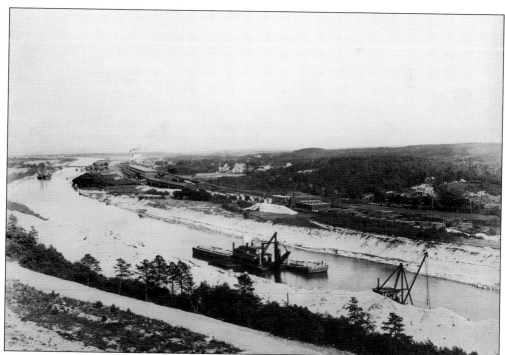

Two dredges work in front of the Keith Car and Manufacturing Works at Sagamore around 1913. *Harper's Weekly* lamented that the canal would change Cape Cod forever: "Exit Cape Cod's seafaring and cranberry-raising folk, along with many of its historic spots and buildings. These cherished landmarks are falling before the steam-shovel and gravel-train of the canal builders."

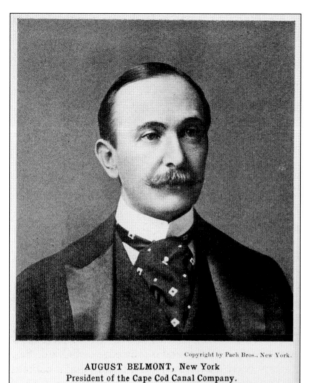

Copyright by Pach Bros., New York.

AUGUST BELMONT, New York
President of the Cape Cod Canal Company.

August Perry Belmont finally brought the Cape Cod Canal to completion. A New York banker and Thoroughbred horse owner and investor (Man o' War and Belmont Park, respectively), Belmont completed the first New York subway line in 1904. The canal was a personal quest for Belmont: his maternal grandfather, Commodore Matthew Perry, was born on the Perry farm in the path of the canal.

William Barclay Parsons (1859–1932) was chief engineer for the Cape Cod Canal. A graduate of Columbia University, Parsons began his career in railroad design. He supervised the construction of a 1,000-mile-long railroad corridor in China through areas previously closed to Westerners. Parsons's skill and ingenuity as chief engineer made possible the construction of the New York subway system, where he worked closely with August Perry Belmont. His engineering firm continues today as Parsons Brinckerhoff.

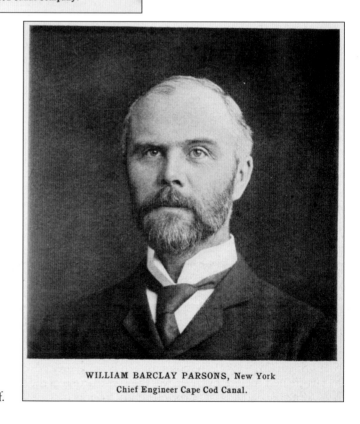

WILLIAM BARCLAY PARSONS, New York
Chief Engineer Cape Cod Canal.

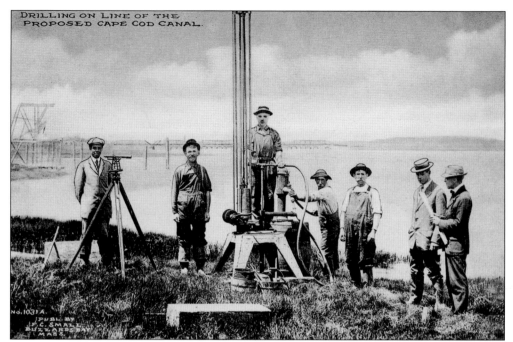

DRILLING ON LINE OF THE PROPOSED CAPE COD CANAL.

One of William Parsons's crews conducts test borings in the sand on the edge of Buzzards Bay, next to the Buttermilk Bay Channel. Parsons worried that the glacial terrain might contain quicksand, hard clay, large boulders, or other significant barriers. While initial suspicions of quicksand proved unfounded, the presence of large buried boulders became an ongoing problem. (Photograph by Fred C. Small.)

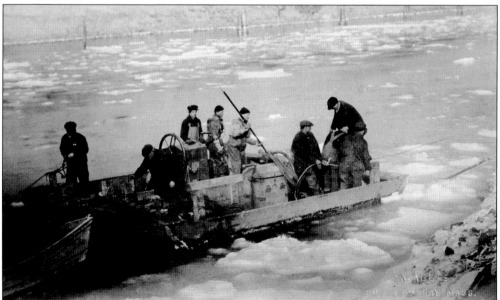

Bundled against the cold, workmen struggle with equipment in the canal's icy waters. Photographer Fred C. Small (1875–1961), the postmaster in Bourne, tirelessly documented many aspects of town life. His greatest subject, however, was the construction of the Cape Cod Canal. (Photograph by Fred C. Small; courtesy of Bourne Historical Society.)

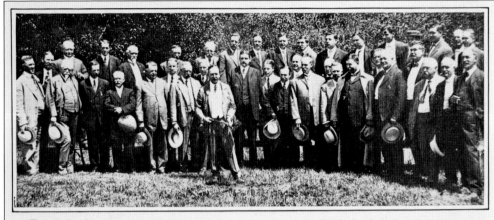

Mr. August Belmont digging the first spadeful of earth to begin the work of completing the great Cape Cod Ship Canal before a group of his guests
1. EX-GOVERNOR WARFIELD OF MARYLAND. 2. MR. KLAPP, ENGINEER (ASSISTANT OF WILLIAM B. PARSONS). 3. AUGUST BELMONT. 4. DEWITT C. FLANAGAN. 5.
AUGUST BELMONT, JR. 6. A. FURST, CONTRACTOR. 7. L. F. LOREE, PRESIDENT OF THE DELAWARE AND HUDSON RAILROAD COMPANY. 8. ROBERT BACON, FORMER
SECRETARY OF STATE. 9. M. J. DEGNON, PRESIDENT OF THE DEGNON CAPE COD CONSTRUCTION COMPANY

At the Perry family farm in Bourne on June 22, 1909, August Perry Belmont (center, with silver shovel) pauses after turning over the first shovelful of dirt, inaugurating digging for the Cape Cod Canal. Perry is surrounded by investors, contractors, and invited dignitaries, including former Maryland governor Edwin Warfield, for whom a dredge was named. (Photograph by Fred C. Small.)

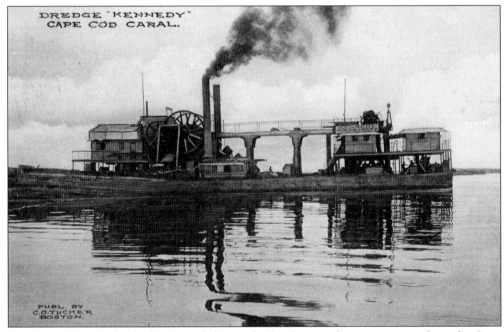

On August 2, 1909, the dredge *Kennedy* began the first large-scale excavation work on the Cape Cod Canal, deepening the channel in Buzzards Bay. The *Kennedy* was a ladder dredge that used a continuous series of buckets.

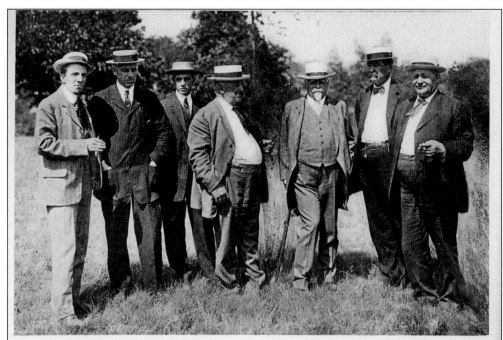

H. W. DURHAM Resident Engineer.	A. S. ACKERMAN Engineer Eastern Division.	EX. GOV. EDWIN WARFIELD of Maryland.	F. A. FURST Vice-President, Degnon Cape Canal Construction Company
EUGENE KLAPP Deputy Chief Engineer Cape Cod Construction Company.	C. M. THOMPSON In Charge of Real Estate Dept.		M. J DEGNON Pres., Degnon Cape Cod Canal Construction Company.

Shown here in 1909, these men were instrumental in building the Cape Cod Canal. Henry Welles Durham and A.S. Ackerman (first and third from left) had worked with William Parsons on the Panama Canal; Parsons left that job when his suggestion of a sea-level canal was rejected in favor of locks. Charles M. Thompson (center) had been assistant engineer to Frederick A. Lockwood in the 1880s and stayed on as a local agent for the canal thereafter.

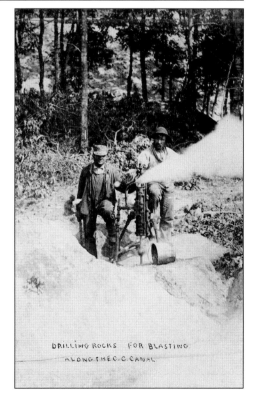

DRILLING ROCKS FOR BLASTING ALONG THE C. C. CANAL

Just as important as the engineers were the hundreds of workers who labored in difficult conditions to build the canal. These men are drilling into one of the larger boulders in the canal's path with a steam drill. They used the drill to break rocks apart or to make a cavity to hold an explosive charge.

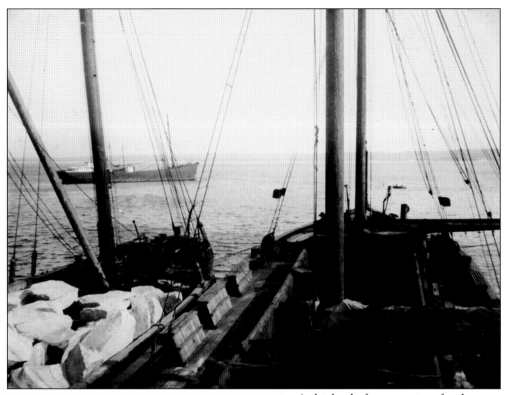

A shipload of stone arrives for the breakwater. Michael J. Degnon, the New York subcontractor who built the Fourth Avenue Subway in New York for August Belmont, headed up the breakwater construction. The difficult work drove Degnon to bankruptcy in 1912.

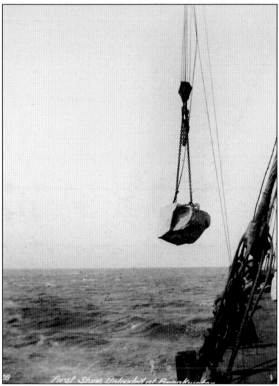

On June 19, 1909, the schooner *Annie F. Lewis* dropped the first piece of Maine granite into Cape Cod Bay to begin the eastern breakwater. The following spring, after a dissatisfying season of antiquated transports and fraudulently short loads, canal builders fired their stone supplier and contracted directly with Cape Ann granite quarries.

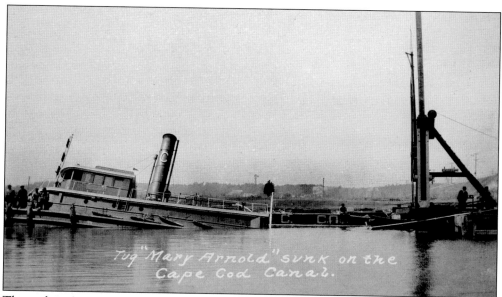

The tugboat *Mary Arnold* began work on the Cape Cod Canal in 1909 but sank in 1913. On the back of this postcard, dated June 18, 1913, someone has written, "This is a close view. I am not in this one. Got her up and pumped out today [and] will tow to Boston or some other dry dock tomorrow."

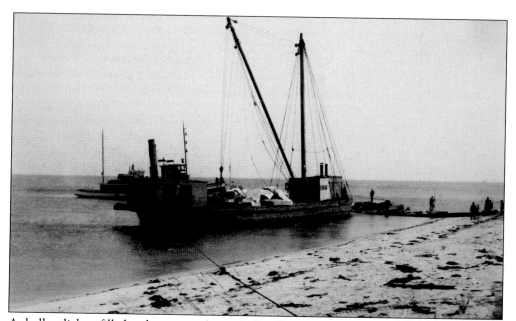

A shallow lighter filled with stone works on the breakwater near the Sandwich beach in summer 1909. On July 11, 1909, the *Boston Herald* reported that 300 feet of breakwater were visible at low tide and that six schooners, including the *S.M. Bird* and the *Mystic*, had deposited 5,000 tons of stone during the previous week.

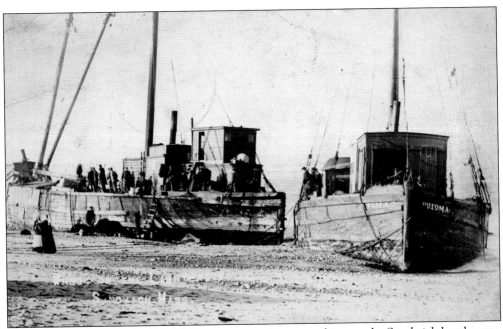

On November 8, 1909, a sudden nor'easter surprised crews working on the Sandwich breakwater. The lighters *Ben Franklin* and *Potomac* were unloading rock from the schooner *Elizabeth Gilbert*. The lighters tore loose from their moorings and eventually crashed to shore, their crews terrified but not seriously injured. The crews stripped the lighters for salvage before a second storm on November 21 tore their hulks to pieces. A third storm on November 29 almost sank the dredge *General MacKenzie*. The next day, a man from Sandwich mailed the above postcard to James Driscoll in Provincetown: "Dear Jim, How are you after your trip across the pond? Every one was on top of all the hills and churches looking at the dredge. I'll bet you was scared." Driscoll was a crewman aboard the *General MacKenzie*, which had made it safely to winter harbor in Provincetown.

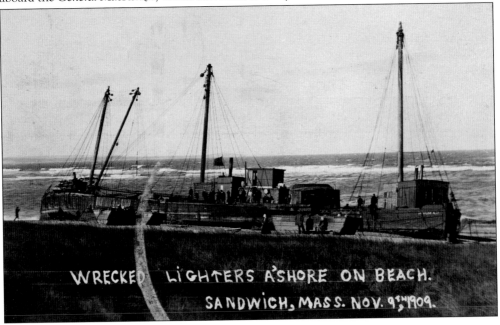

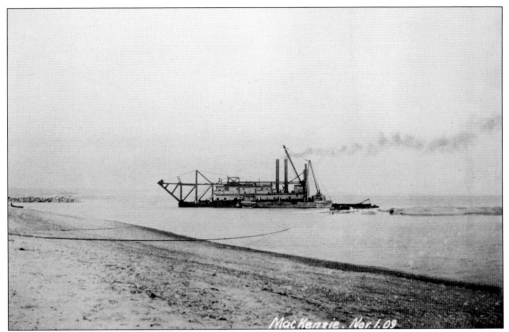

The hydraulic dredge *General MacKenzie* first arrived in Sandwich on October 16, 1909, for a brief period of work. Her crew of 16, though, spent most of their time traveling back and forth to the harbor at Provincetown—a dozen times—before the November storms ended the season. The dredge managed only eight full days of work in 1909.

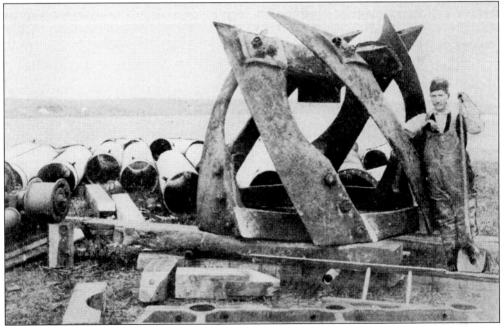

With a cutter larger than a man, the *General MacKenzie* made good progress in the spring of 1910, beginning digging in April in Lockwood's Ditch. Cape Cod Canal historian William James Reid noted that the cutter would still break down "intermittently as its blades clogged on rocks, trees, stumps, and even the vertebrae of a whale."

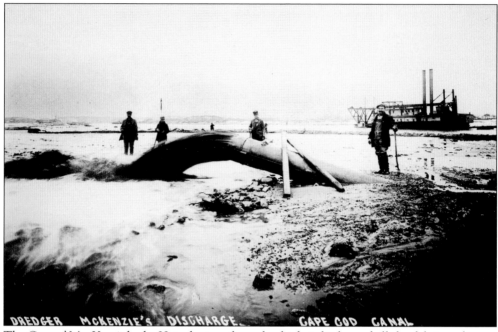

The *General MacKenzie* had a 22-inch pipe, through which it discharged all the debris and water its blade churned up. Much of the crew's time was spent laying and relaying the lengths of pipe, 500 feet total, as the dredge moved forward.

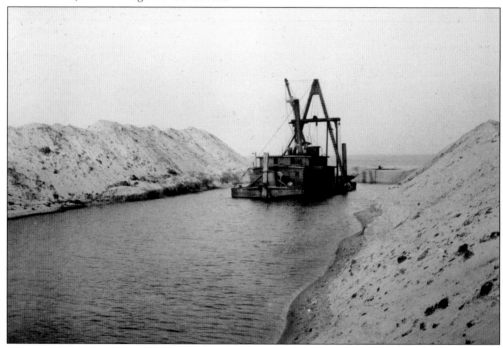

The small dredge *Nahant*, which began work on January 24, 1910, cleared the way for the *General MacKenzie*. Crews waited until high tide to float and pull the *Nahant* across the Scusset marshes into Lockwood's Ditch. The *Nahant* dug until April, opening a path to the sea with its long boom and small "orange peel" bucket.

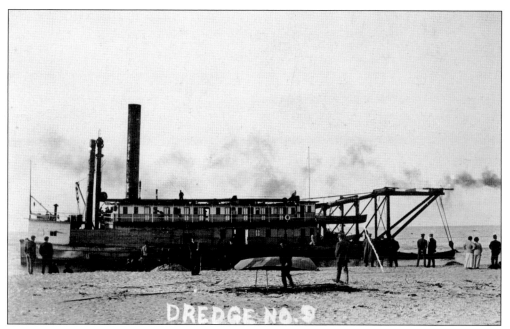

Dredge No. 9 was a hydraulic dredge that followed the General MacKenzie into Lockwood's Ditch in 1910. Since it could not dig as deep as the General MacKenzie, which could reach 23 feet, Dredge No. 9 moved ahead of it in the channel, digging down 17 feet.

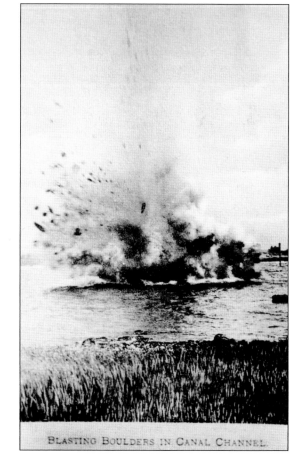

BLASTING BOULDERS IN CANAL CHANNEL.

This creatively enhanced postcard shows one of the countless explosions that reduced larger boulders in the channel into pieces small enough to excavate.

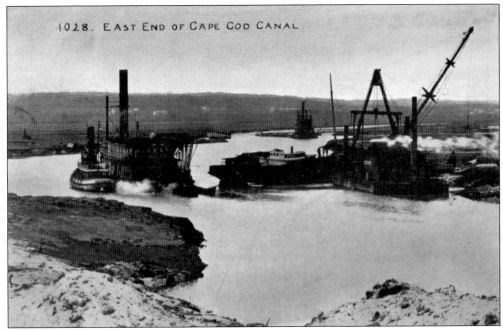

1028. EAST END OF CAPE COD CANAL.

This view, postmarked from Sagamore on August 15, 1910, shows half a dozen vessels at work on the eastern end of the canal, including two tugboats and three dredges; presumably, the *Dredge No. 9*, the *General MacKenzie*, and the *Nahant* are from left to right.

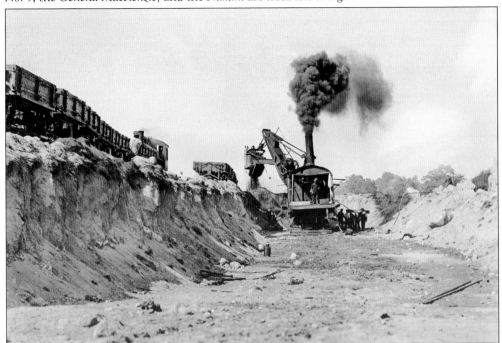

This 1910 photograph shows a large steam shovel belching a cloud of smoke as it carves out the canal floor. The steam shovel loaded sand and dirt into railroad cars on movable tracks. While the dredges worked at both ends of the canal, workers began cutting down the hills in the middle. In 1909, one of their first jobs was to remove the graveyard at Bournedale.

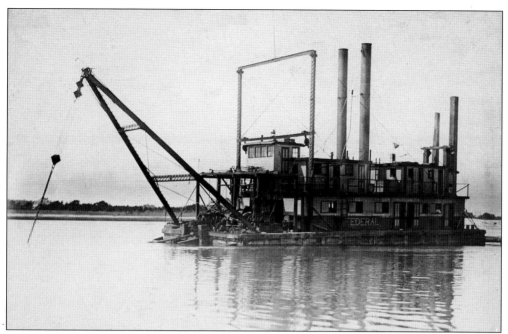

In 1911, the dredge *Federal* began working on the channel at the canal's western end, in the long Buzzards Bay approach, replacing the dredge *Warren*. While progress was easy to see on the eastern end, where the dredges had reached the Sandwich/Bourne town line by the end of 1910, work to the west was mostly concealed under water.

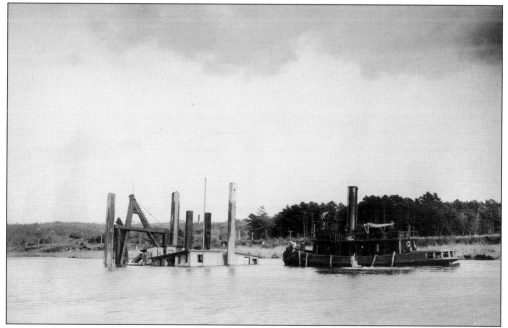

In May 1914, the dredge *National* sank in the canal; its crewmembers swam safely ashore. The *National*, along with the *Capitol* and *International*, were old dipper dredges that had been added to the ragtag canal fleet early in 1911. The contractor patched the *National*'s leak, refloated it, and put it back to work.

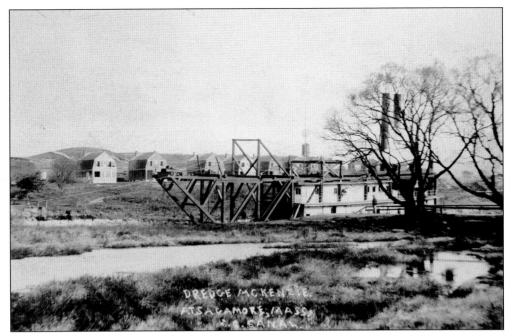

In April 1911, the dredge *General MacKenzie* started to work again, deepening the channel created in the previous months by the three dipper dredges. The gambrel-roofed cottages of Sagamore are visible across the canal to the north.

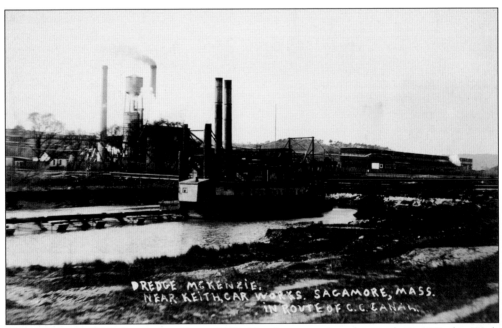

Shown here in 1911, the dredge *General MacKenzie* approaches the Keith Car Works. With the founding of the Boston and Sandwich Glass Company in 1825, Sandwich became the industrial center of Cape Cod. The Keith Car Works, founded in 1846 in Scusset (later known as West Sandwich and then Sagamore), was one of many factories that sprang up nearby in the subsequent decades.

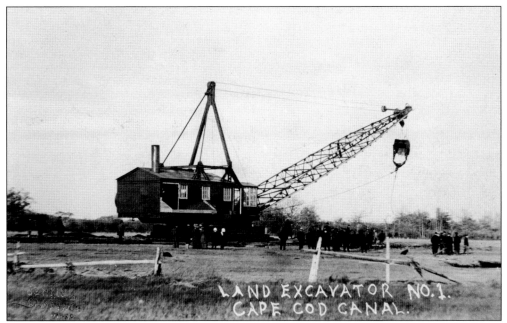

Early in 1910, two ungainly land excavators arrived from Chicago, first clearing a path through the Scusset marshes for the dredge *Nahant* to enter Lockwood's Ditch. *Land Excavator No. 1's* 100-foot boom and large scoop looked impressive, but the machine was difficult to move and unsuited for the marshy conditions along the canal.

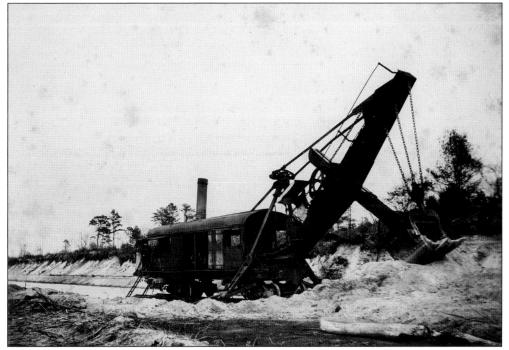

Much more efficient was the smaller steam shovel *Wilson*, which also worked on excavating the central sections of the canal's path. The Wilson and English Construction Company, subcontractors, started digging near Bournedale in July 1912.

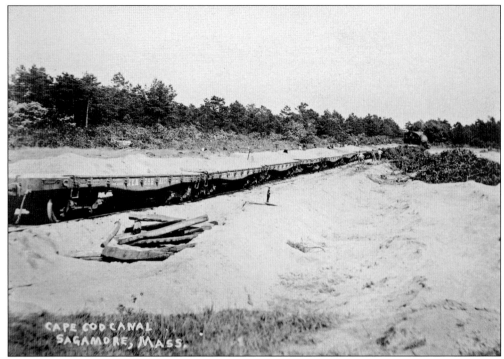

Workers had to lay temporary tracks numerous times as the steam shovels removed the sand near Sagamore around 1912. Here, the sand has been loaded onto a long line of flatbed cars.

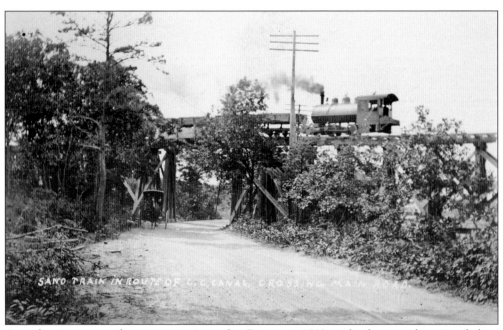

A sand train on a trestle crosses a main road in Bourne in 1912, with a horse and carriage below. The Wilson and English Construction Company used four narrow-gauge locomotives and several dozen cars to haul away sand and debris from the canal path.

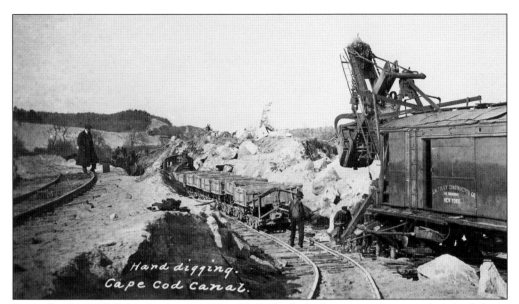

Crews for the E.W. Foley Company of New York check the bracing on a steam shovel, while an engine and a string of side-dumping railroad cars await filling. Foley crews arrived at the canal in August 1912, cutting through the valley between Bournedale and Bourne.

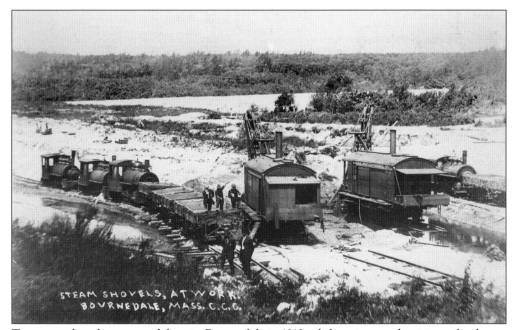

Two steam shovels are at work here in Bournedale in 1912, while trains stand waiting to haul away the sand. The steam shovels were the most efficient element of canal construction, easily dealing with the boulders that clogged the dredges and stopped all work until their demolition.

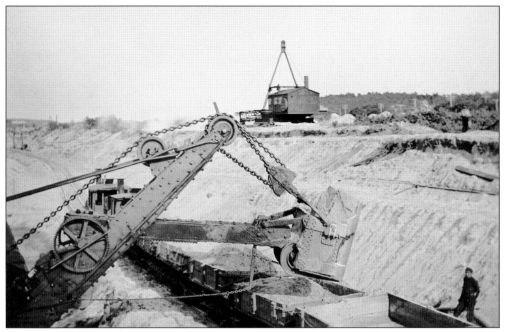

A steam shovel prepares to drop a load of sand into a railroad side-dump car. The Furst-Clark Construction Company, the main excavation subcontractors, began dry digging too late to meet their deadlines. Frank A. Furst (1845–1934) of Baltimore, president of the company, had dredged the canals that opened the Florida Everglades to development.

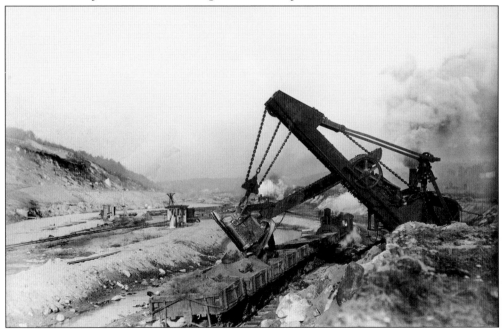

In 1909, chief engineer William Parsons started asking the contractors to secure more steam shovels for dry digging, such as this one working near Bournedale in 1913. The delay in bringing in additional equipment cost the project dearly; Parsons estimated later that the canal could have been completed two years earlier if his advice had been followed.

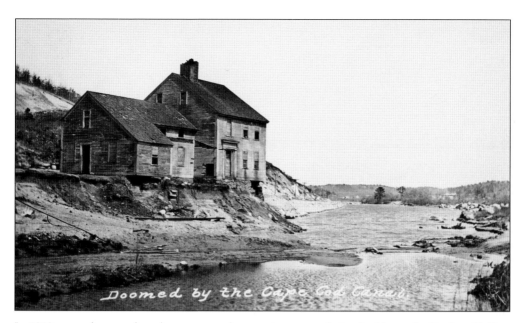

Doomed by the Cape Cod Canal

In 1913, several steam shovels were at work removing most of what had been the Reuben Collins farm, on the banks of the Monument (Manomet) River between Bourne and Bournedale. The river, which begins in Great Herring Pond in Plymouth, was diverted to the Cape Cod Bay. Pumps helped extend the dry digging 15 feet below sea level. The Collins farmhouse, shown partially on the left in the photograph below, was eventually relocated farther from the channel.

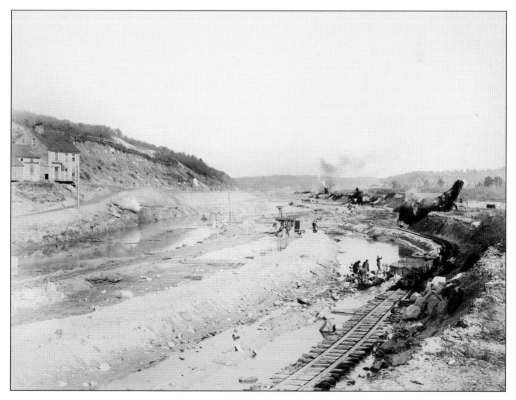

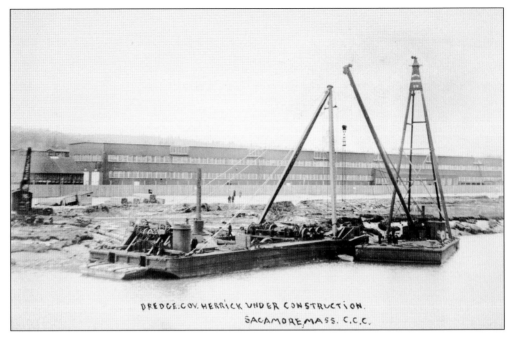

DREDGE.GOV. HERRICK UNDER CONSTRUCTION.
SACAMORE.MASS. C.C.C.

Dredging efforts improved significantly after 1911, when the Furst-Clark Construction Company hired the American Locomotive Company to design and build two new dredges. Assembled in Sagamore near the Keith Car Works, the *Governor Herrick* was christened with champagne on March 31, 1912. But its maiden voyage (below) was short; after sliding 10 feet, it stopped and could not be moved farther, even when pulled by a tug. Journalists, dignitaries, and the small crowd finally dispersed. Freed a week later, the *Governor Herrick* did not actually begin work until July 2, 1912, when its superstructure and equipment had been installed.

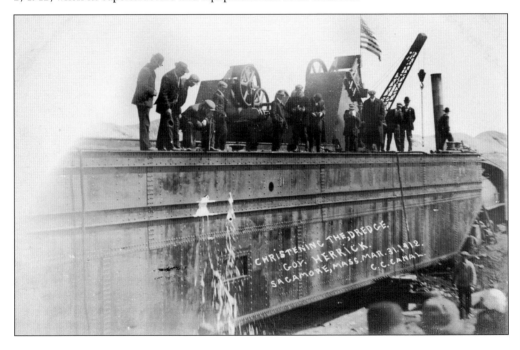

CHRISTENING THE DREDGE.
GOV. HERRICK.
SAGAMORE,MASS MAR.31,1912.
C.C.CANAL.

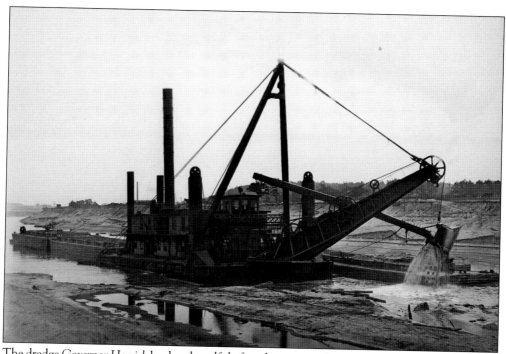

The dredge *Governor Herrick* loads a shovelful of mud onto one of a string of barges near Bournedale. When it came to the Cape Cod Canal, the *Governor Herrick* was the largest dredge known. Its 10-cubic-yard shovel could excavate 100,000 cubic yards of dirt in a month.

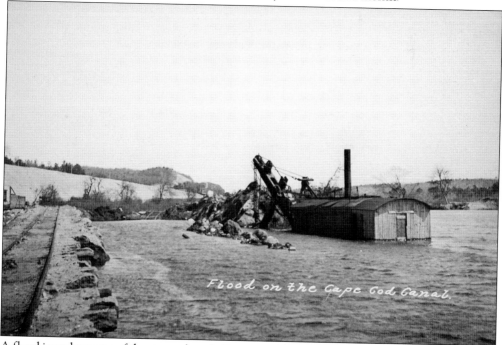

Flood on the Cape Cod Canal.

A flood inundates one of the steam shovels. Because of the scope and complexities of its operation, the canal had its share of accidents. Six men died during its construction, mostly by drowning; their names were not recorded.

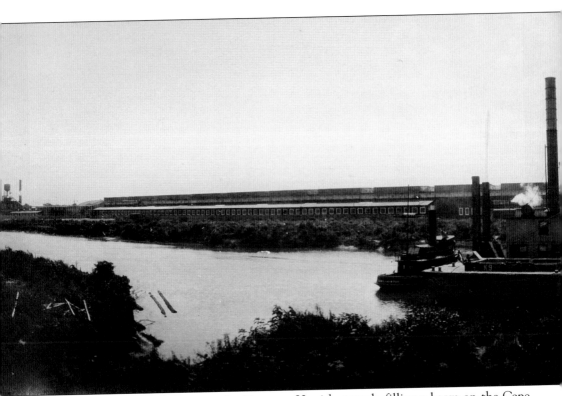

A panoramic photograph captures the *Governor Herrick* at work, filling a barge on the Cape Cod Canal, in August 1912. The Keith Car Works plant, a landmark on the southeast bank of the canal, provided a dramatic backdrop for many photographs. Begun as a blacksmith and wheelwright shop in 1829 and incorporated in 1846 to manufacture carriages, the factory evolved with the times. It produced miners' tools for the California Gold Rush, Conestoga wagons for the

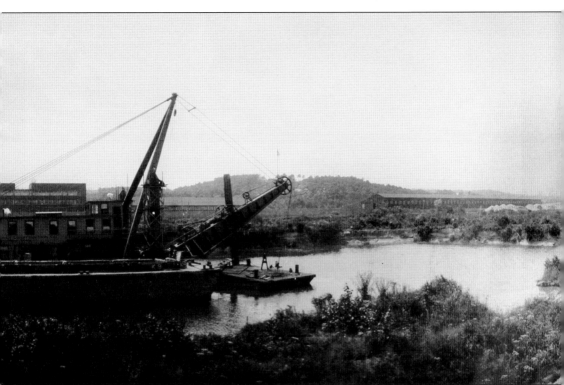

Oregon Trail, countless railroad cars, and specialized cars for New York City's elevated railway and subway. In 1907, Eben S.S. Keith, grandson of the founder, rebuilt the plant with concrete-footed steel buildings. By the 1920s, Keith Manufacturing was the largest single employer in Barnstable County, its 300 workers mostly living across the canal in Sagamore. The plant closed in the 1930s and was torn down to expand the canal in 1935.

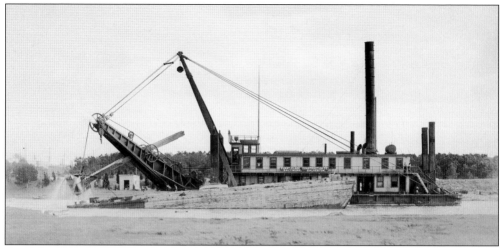

Completed several months after the nearly identical *Governor Herrick*, the dredge *Governor Warfield* is shown here on its first day of operation, August 28, 1912. The *Governor Warfield* started digging just west of the Bourne Bridge, working eastward toward its twin in the channel five miles to the east.

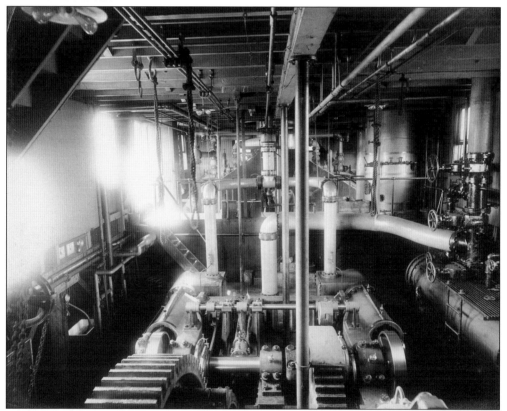

The engine room of the *Governor Warfield* dredge was a complex place, with 12 separate engines operating various independent systems, including a 57-foot boom, which could dig 40 feet deep, and the pair of 70-foot long spuds, which could be sunk into the mud to hold the dredge in place. A crew of 24 men ran the dredge, each working daily on one of two 12-hour shifts.

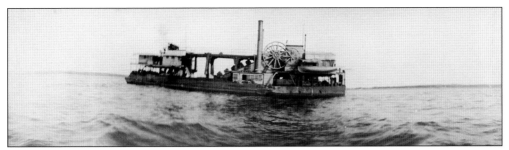

A ladder dredge, likely the *Kennedy*, is at work in Buzzards Bay in 1912. The *Kennedy,* though it worked only in summer, excavated over a million cubic yards of material all together. At the end of 1911, a total of 10 dredges and 15 other vessels, including tugboats and scows, were working on the Buzzards Bay end of the canal.

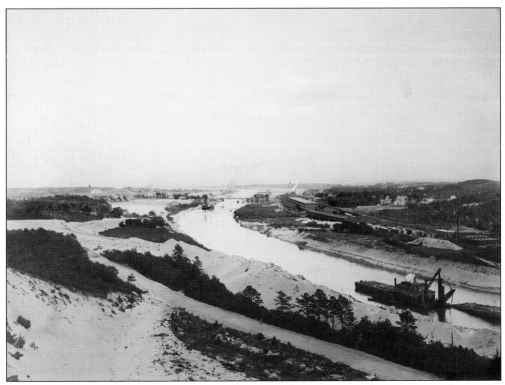

The dredge *Governor Herrick* passes the Keith Car Works at Sagamore late in 1912, widening the channel as it goes. Although much of the canal has yet to be completed, this hilltop view looking east from Bournedale shows it taking shape from the Sagamore Bridge out to Cape Cod Bay.

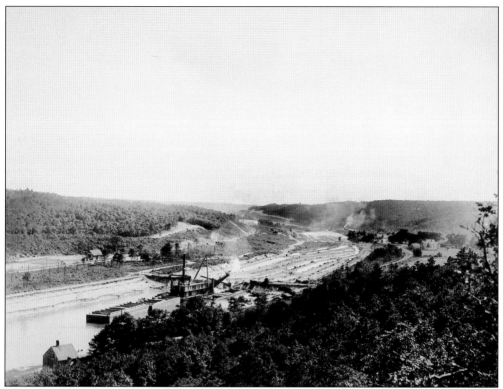

Looking west from a vantage point close to the previous view, this photograph shows the *Governor Herrick* cutting through the roadway connecting the Bournedale railroad station (visible to its left on the far bank) with Bournedale village (to the right) late in 1912. The canal builders provided a ferry between the two banks for several years. A mile or more farther down the valley, steam shovels belch smoke as they work at Collins Farm.

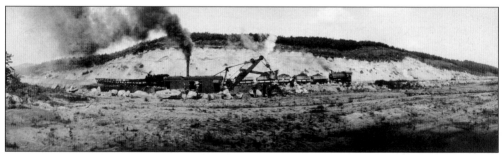

This section from a panoramic photograph, taken in August 1912, shows steam shovels cutting through the valley. A nearly full line of railroad cars awaits its last loads to the right, while another string of empty cars sits to the left. The rows of stone along each side of the shovel's trench were glacial erratic boulders and fragments set aside for riprap on the canal banks.

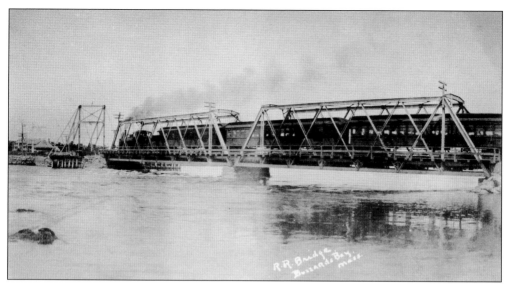

Shown here about 1906 before work began on the Cape Cod Canal, this is one of two railroad bridges near the mouth of the Monument River. The Woods Hole Line crossed at Buzzards Bay and followed the coast of Buzzards Bay south. Close by, just upriver in Bourne, the second railroad bridge carried the Old Colony Railroad across the Monument River, where it continued northeastward to Sandwich and Yarmouth.

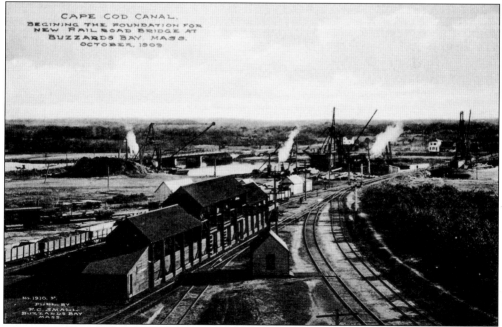

The replacement railroad bridge across the Monument River, used by both the Sandwich and Woods Hole railroad lines, was one of the first elements of the Cape Cod Canal to be finished. Work had begun on the foundations of the new bridge by October 1909, as shown in this view looking east from Buzzards Bay. Upriver to the left is the highway bridge in Buzzards Bay, which would be demolished. (Photograph by Fred C. Small.)

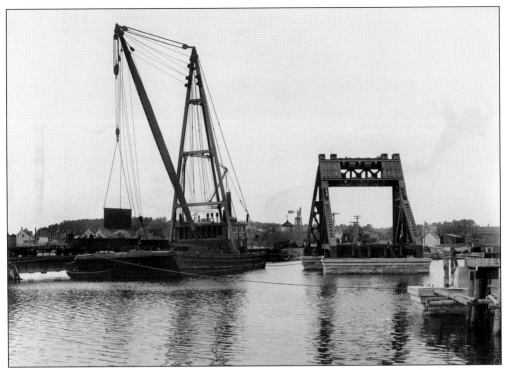

The vessel *Capitol*, working for the Merritt and Chapman Derrick and Wrecking Company, unloads steel for the new Buzzards Bay railroad bridge in summer 1910. The steel arrived on the site by railroad cars, here parked on the old Buzzards Bay Bridge. The company finished the superstructure of the new bridge by September 20.

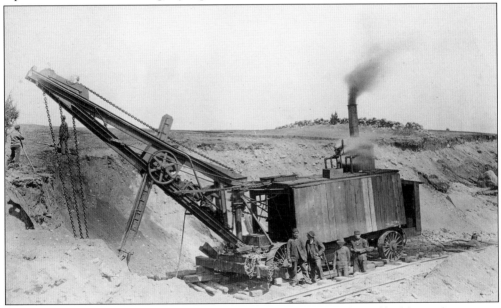

While bridge construction moved relatively quickly, rerouting the tracks and building infrastructure caused many delays. Here, a steam shovel digs into a bank for one of the approaches to a new Cape Cod Canal bridge in 1910 or 1911.

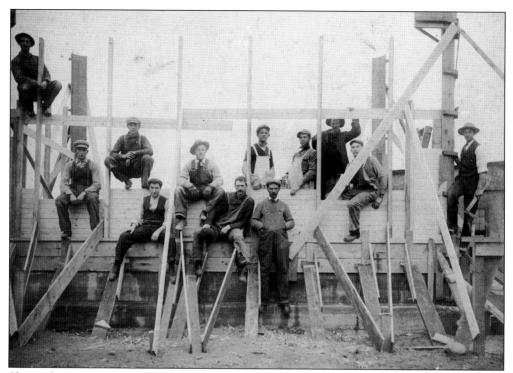

Shown here in 1910, workers take a photograph break during the construction of the new signal box at Buzzards Bay Station for the New York, New Haven & Hartford Railroad. Some of the carpenters are wearing their tool aprons, and the man at the far right still clutches his carpenter's square.

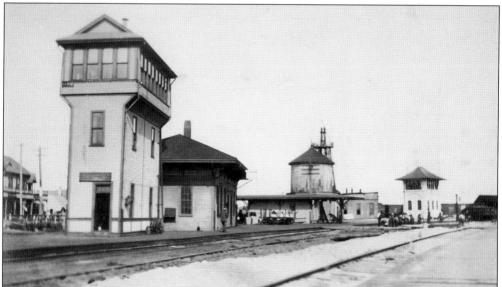

In 1912, the railroad station at Buzzards Bay was a confusing jumble of old and new. The old signal box (also known as an interlocking tower) appears in the left foreground, while the new tower stands at the far right. Interlocking towers allowed a signalman to monitor and control train switching for several lines from a single location.

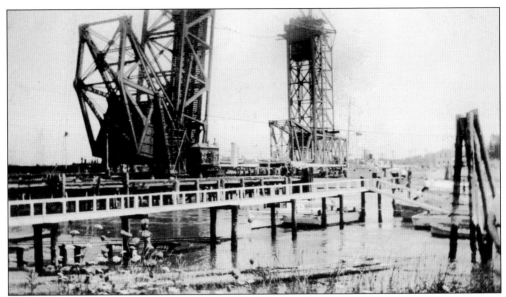

This photograph shows the Buzzards Bay Railroad Bridge shortly after its completion. Now double-tracked, the bridge opened to train traffic in November 1911, taking the place of both the Buzzards Bay and Bourne railroad bridges.

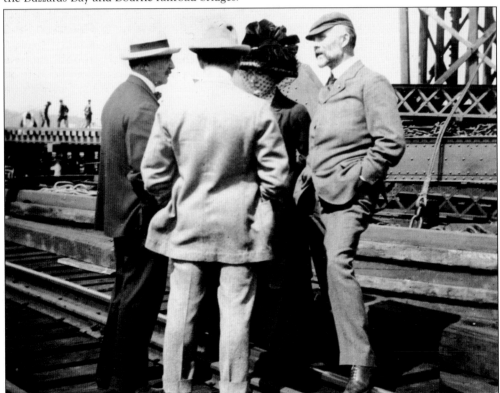

Late in 1911, canal planners confer on an inspection tour at the Buzzards Bay Railroad Bridge. From left to right are August Perry Belmont; his son Raymond Belmont; August Belmont's second wife, Eleanor Robson Belmont; and William Barclay Parsons.

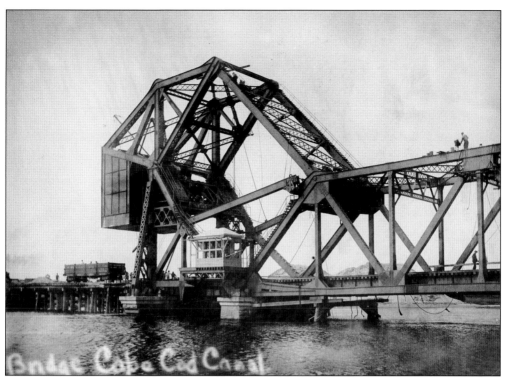

The new Buzzards Bay Railroad Bridge of 1910 was a Strauss trunnion bascule bridge. Its single span, 160 feet in length, pivoted on its foundation at the northern end. Lifted by two 65-horsepower motors, the bridge took a minute and a half to open. The key to its technology was the enormous counterweight, a steel box filled with 1,200 tons of concrete. Train service to Sandwich was restored in September 1912.

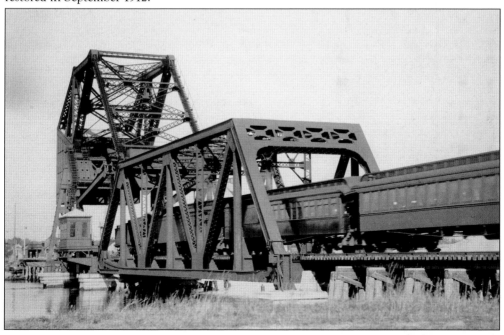

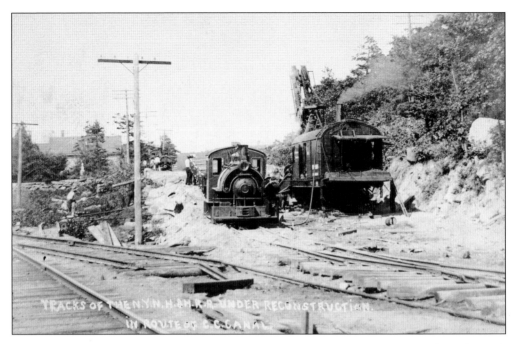

These 1911 postcards show the machinery required to relocate the train tracks through much of the valley. Both depict the *No. 3* railroad steam shovel owned by subcontractor Wilson and English and manufactured by the Bucyrus Company of South Milwaukee. The inscription on the back of the top card reads "A part of the job. The reconstruction here is a mile long with one or two fairly heavy cuts." On the other card, the sender wrote his father, "Here is a picture of the steam shovel at our job. Note your son on the left working. Don't forget that c[hec]k if you haven't sent it."

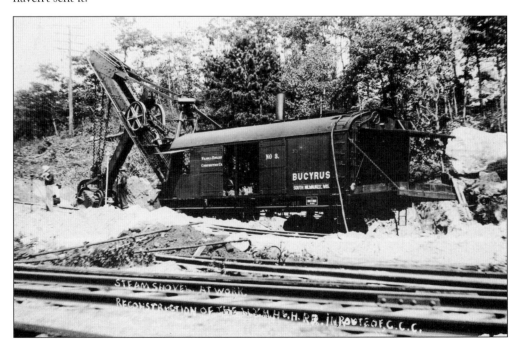

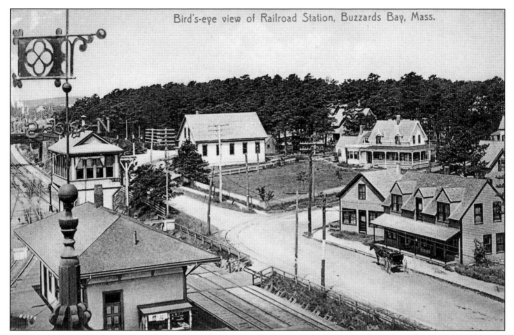

This 1908 postcard shows the railroad station and surrounding neighborhood at Buzzards Bay, about to be transformed by the Cape Cod Canal. The weather vane in the foreground was located on the roof of the water tower; the buildings immediately beyond are the old depot and signal box, all soon to be torn down. (Photograph by Fred C. Small)

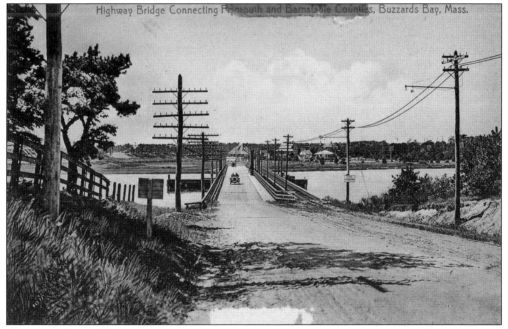

Cars cross the old Bourne Bridge, one of two nearby roadway bridges dismantled for the Cape Cod Canal. The bridge had a sidetrack for street trolley cars from the New Bedford & Onset Street Railway, which operated from New Bedford through Bourne and as far south as Monument Beach from 1901 until 1926. (Photograph by Fred C. Small.)

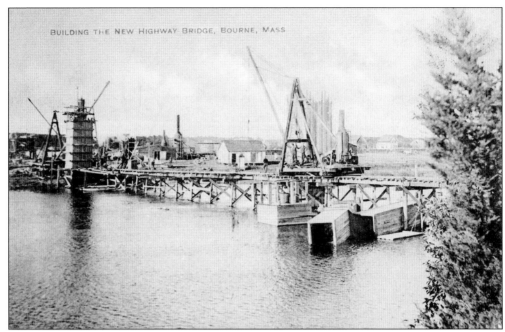

In August 1910, the Merritt and Chapman Derrick and Wrecking Company began work on a replacement highway bridge in Bourne. This Scherzer double-leaf rolling lift bridge was 30 feet across, extra wide to accommodate the trolley tracks. Each of the electrically operated cantilevered leaves was 80 feet long, with a total bridge span of 729 feet. The bed was 41 feet above sea level, allowing smaller boats to pass under it. The Bourne Bridge was finished in May 1911. The first electric trolley crossed it in June, and vehicle traffic followed in October. Below, in 1912, the newly built dredge *Governor Warfield* deepened the 142-foot-wide channel between the bridge's piers. The railroad bridge can be seen in the distance.

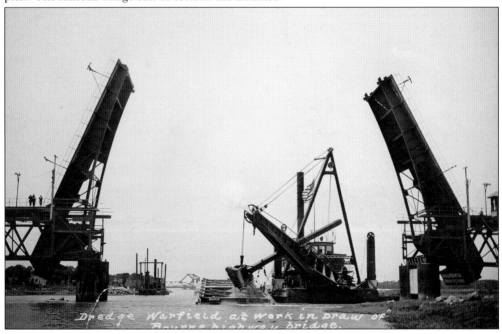

56

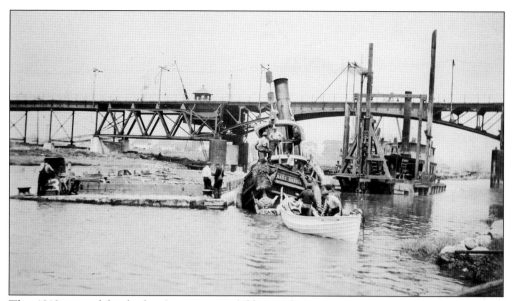

This 1912 view of the dredge *Governor Warfield* at work near the Bourne Bridge is perhaps more interesting for the small boats and their crews in the foreground. The tugboat *Mary Arnold* is docked next to what appears to be a construction barge and is being approached by a rowboat.

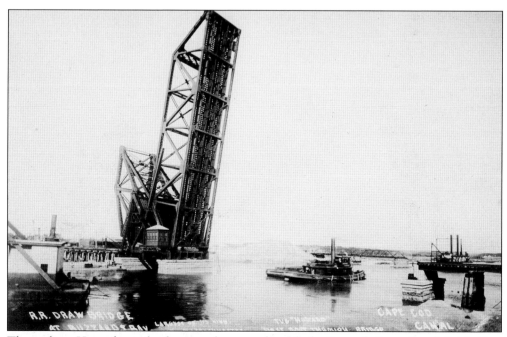

The tugboat *Howard* was the first vessel to pass through the Buzzards Bay railroad drawbridge, presumably in 1911.

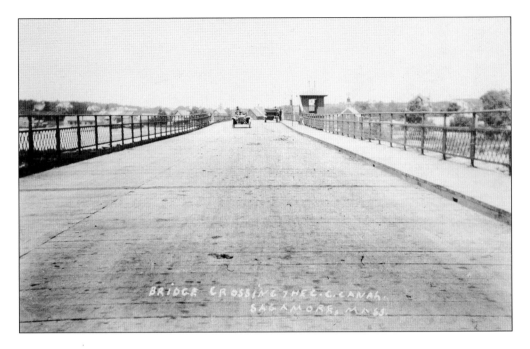

The Cape Cod Construction Company opened the last of its three new bridges, the highway bridge at Sagamore, in February 1913. The basic design was almost identical to the Bourne Bridge, except that it was narrower because it had no trolley track. The Sagamore Bridge replaced a small bridge over Scusset Creek on the old Plymouth Road, discontinued in November 1911. The photograph below shows a dredge (right) beginning to chew through the roadbed. The company built a temporary wooden drawbridge for Sagamore workers to use until it finished the new bridge.

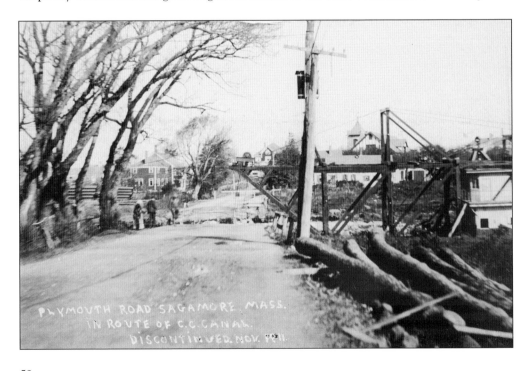

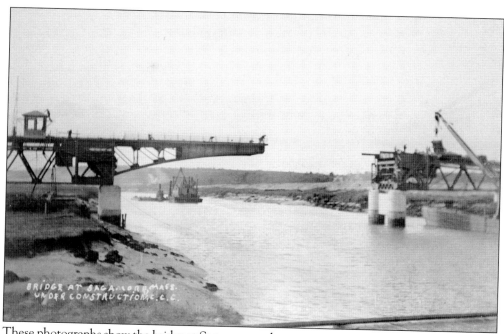

These photographs show the bridge at Sagamore under construction in 1912 (above, looking west from the temporary bridge) and several years after completion (below, looking east, with the Keith Car Works in the background). All three of these early bridges were destroyed just two decades later when the Cape Cod Canal was widened. But their interesting designs and clear photographic documentation make them worth remembering. (Below, photograph by New England News.)

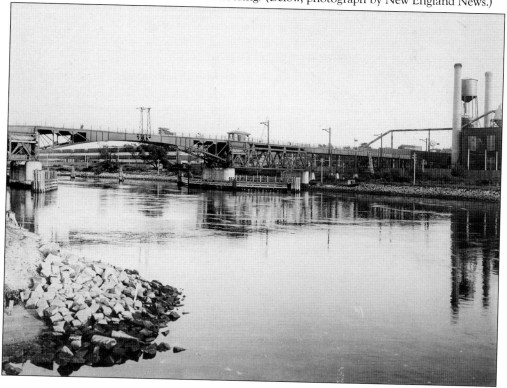

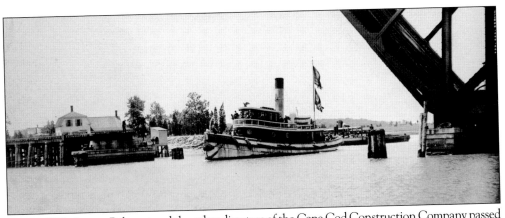

In June 1913, August Belmont and the other directors of the Cape Cod Construction Company passed through the railroad drawbridge on an inspection tour of the canal, now nearing completion.

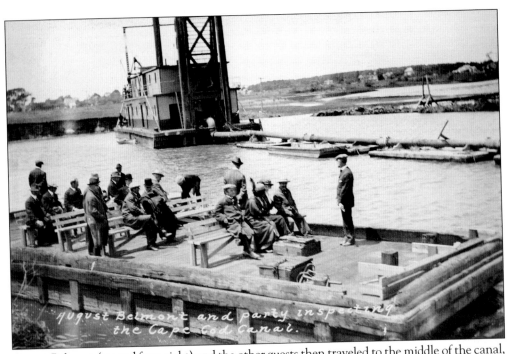

August Belmont (second from right) and the other guests then traveled to the middle of the canal, where the dredge *Federal* was at work. They boarded a scow fitted with benches and listened as William Parsons (far right) explained the progress at each stop. Photographers were invited to all of these carefully staged events in order to generate the best possible publicity. (Photograph by Fred C. Small; courtesy Bourne Historical Society.)

August Perry Belmont's first wife, Elizabeth, had died in Paris in 1898. In 1910, Belmont (right) married again, to Eleanor Robson Belmont (left, 1879–1979), a renowned British actress. Robson was a Broadway star for a decade; George Bernard Shaw wrote the title role in *Major Barbara* for her. She retired from acting upon her marriage, and may be best known today for serving on the board of the Metropolitan Opera and founding the Metropolitan Opera Guild in 1952.

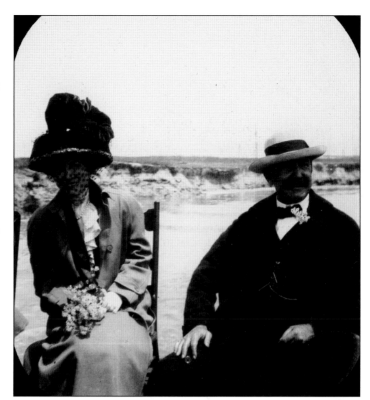

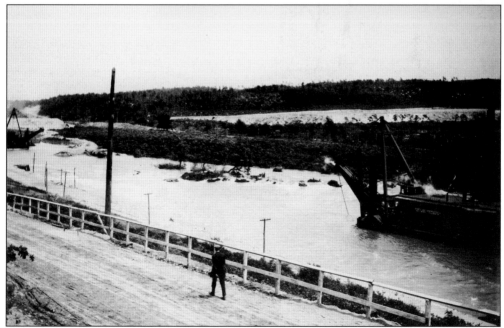

On July 7, 1914, the dredge *Governor Warfield* (right) and the *Governor Herrick* worked toward each other in the open channel near Bournedale. Although the excavation had taken two years longer than planned, the Cape Cod Canal was now one single channel. (Photograph by Fred C. Small; courtesy Bourne Historical Society.)

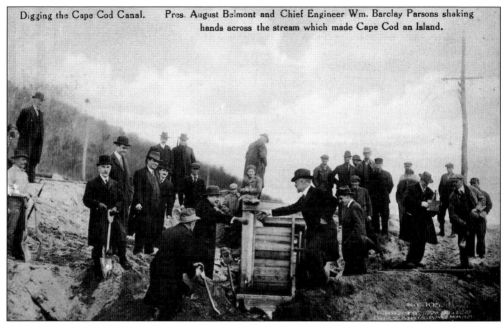

Digging the Cape Cod Canal.   Pres. August Belmont and Chief Engineer Wm. Barclay Parsons shaking hands across the stream which made Cape Cod an Island.

August Belmont conducted another inspection tour of the Cape Cod Canal on April 21, 1914, timed to begin a final publicity campaign for the canal opening. Belmont first staged a "blending of the waters" ceremony, where he poured out together water from two bottles, one holding water from the Cape Cod Bay and the other water from Buzzards Bay. He declared, "May the meeting of these waters bring happiness and prosperity to our country and save some of the misery which the waters of the Cape have caused in the past." With some digging (below), a trickle of tidal water was sent down a sluiceway from one side to the other, and Belmont reached across and shook William Parsons's hand. (Above, photograph by Fred C. Small.)

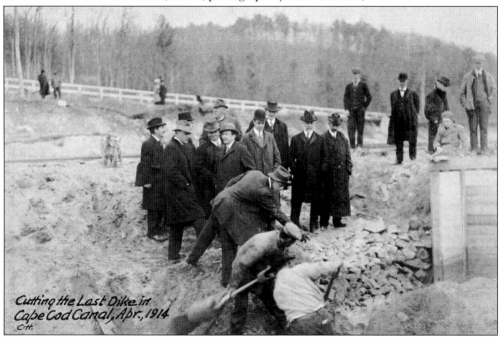

Cutting the Last Dike in Cape Cod Canal, Apr., 1914

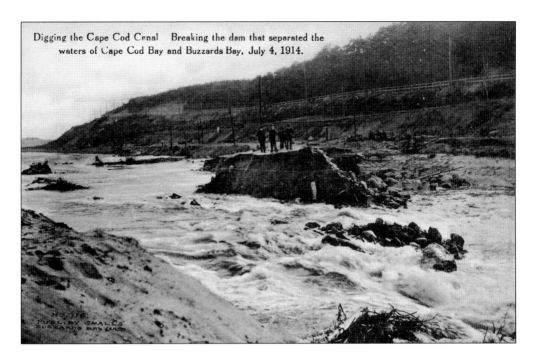

Digging the Cape Cod Canal   Breaking the dam that separated the
waters of Cape Cod Bay and Buzzards Bay, July 4, 1914.

Belmont returned to the canal on July 4, 1914, for a second ceremony. Despite the private objections of some of his contractors, who wanted more time, Belmont ordered workers with shovels to breach the top of Foley's Dyke. As the holiday crowd watched, the tidal waters quickly ripped through most of the dyke. The strong currents, branches, and debris challenged both of the giant dredges, which struggled to maintain their positions in the channel. (Both, photograph by Fred C. Small.)

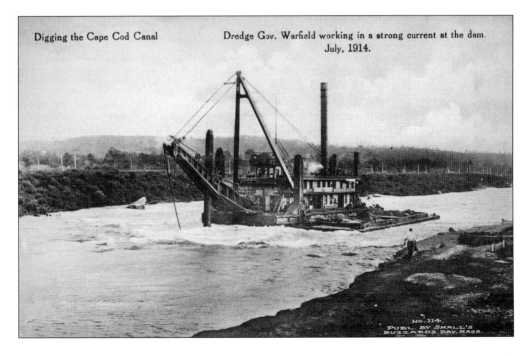

Digging the Cape Cod Canal   Dredge Gov. Warfield working in a strong current at the dam.
July, 1914.

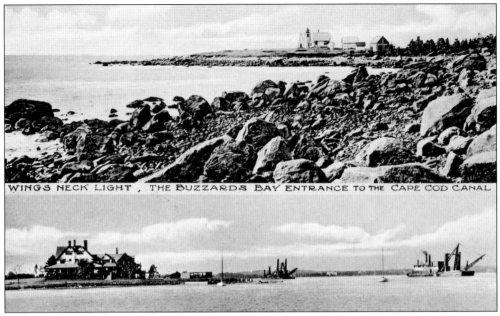

WINGS NECK LIGHT , THE BUZZARDS BAY ENTRANCE TO THE CAPE COD CANAL

Counting the channels cut through Buzzards Bay and the long breakwaters, the Cape Cod Canal was 13 miles long, stretching west to east from Wings Neck Lighthouse, past Gray Gables and the Crow's Nest, past three new bridges and the transformed villages of Bourne and Sandwich, to the long granite breakwaters in Cape Cod Bay. Measured from shore to shore, the channel crossed almost eight miles of land. (Photograph by Cape Cod Camera Craft Company.)

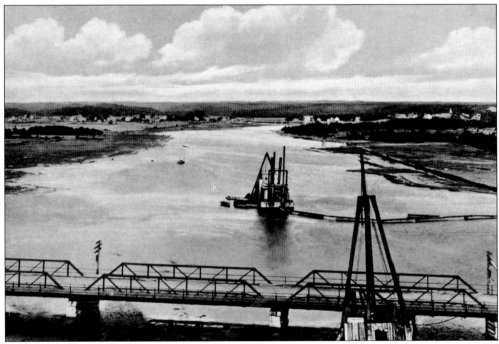

Much of the old Bourne had, indeed, been swept away: houses, depots, roads, bridges, graveyards, and even the Monument River. In its place was an engineering marvel that would struggle to earn its keep. Cape Cod was now an island. (Photograph by Cape Cod Camera Craft Company.)

Three

COMMERCE
THE CANAL OPENS

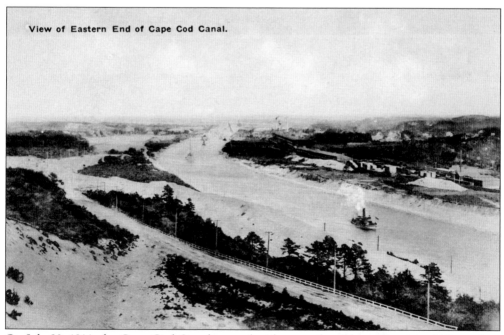

View of Eastern End of Cape Cod Canal.

On July 29, 1914, the Cape Cod Canal opened with a parade of ships. Five years before, when August Belmont turned the first shovelful of dirt on his ancestral farm in Bournedale, he had vowed, "I promise not to desert the task until the last shovelful of dirt has been dug." Although Belmont would not finish the canal to its required specifications for another two years, he still made good on his promise. (Photograph by Fred C. Small.)

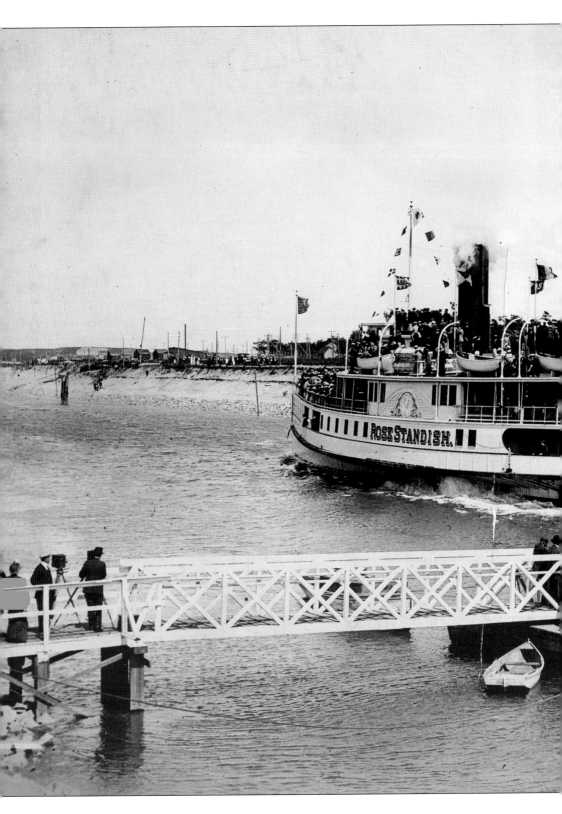

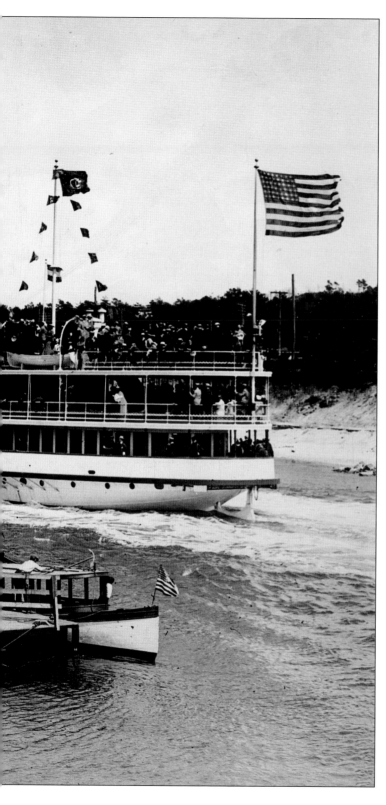

Photographers recorded the opening of the Cape Cod Canal from numerous vantage points, sometimes catching each other in their photographs. August Belmont marked the day by chartering a Boston excursion steamer, the *Rose Standish*. It served as the lead vessel in a squadron of more than two-dozen vessels that carried dignitaries, friends, honored guests, and workers through the new canal. Supporters boarded special trains from Boston, New York, and Newport to New Bedford, from which the squadron departed with great fanfare. Its whistle blasting constantly, the *Rose Standish* cut through the red, white, and blue bunting stretched across the canal at 1:31 p.m. The Cape Cod Canal was officially open.

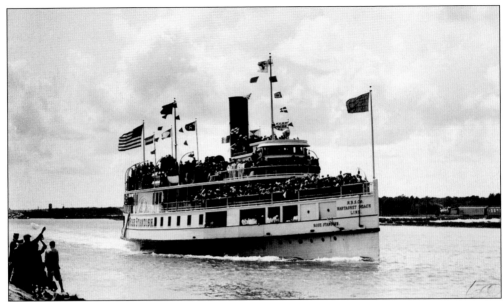

The *Rose Standish*, with 1,200 aboard, led the parade of ships through the length of the canal, At Sandwich, August Belmont's private yacht, *Scout*, pulled alongside the *Rose Standish* so that Belmont, Massachusetts governor David Walsh, and other guests could disembark to attend celebrations in Sandwich. Then the squadron continued out into Cape Cod Bay before turning around to return to the main celebration at Bourne. (Photograph by R. L. Graham.)

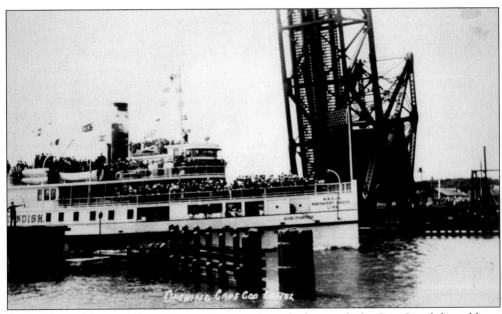

Pushed forward by a swelling tide moving west through the canal, the *Rose Standish* could not slow enough to stop at the pier in Bourne to let off its passengers. Despite its engines churning full astern, it passed the dock and bewildered spectators on shore. Unable to turn around, the *Rose Standish* continued out into Buzzards Bay and safely made the turn. It passed the Buzzards Bay Railroad Bridge a second time on its way to Bourne.

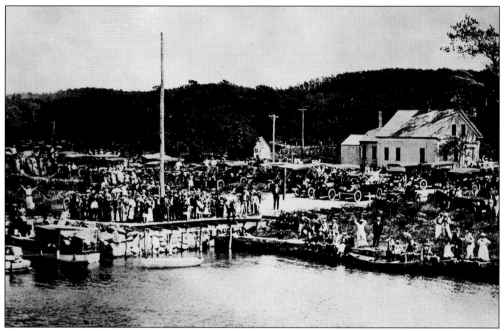

Those waiting at the dock at Bourne were doubly excited to see the *Rose Standish* return safely, so that its guests could join the party Bourne had planned. The expertly organized day should have been a publicity bonanza for the Cape Cod Canal, but on the following day, all newspaper headlines were about the talk of war in Europe.

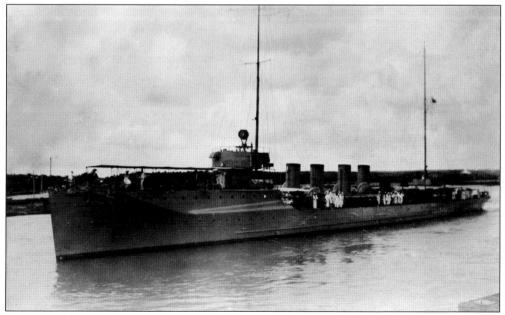

The second boat in the squadron was the US destroyer *McDougal*, one of many governmental ships taking part, including six torpedo boat destroyers and the submarine USS *Wasp*. The revenue cutters *Acushnet* and *Gresham* joined the group at the entrance to the canal, where the *Gresham* hailed them with a 21-gun salute. Aboard the *McDougal* was Assistant Secretary of the Navy (and later president) Franklin Delano Roosevelt.

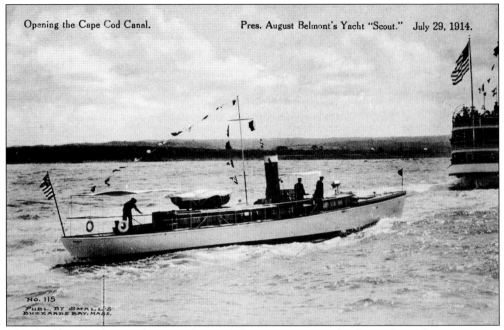

The third boat in the squadron was August Belmont's private yacht, *Scout*, shown here preparing to pull alongside the *Rose Standish* at Sandwich. (Photograph by Fred C. Small.)

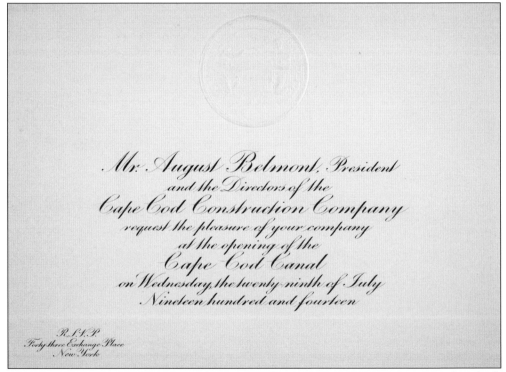

Mr. August Belmont, President
and the Directors of the
Cape Cod Construction Company
request the pleasure of your company
at the opening of the
Cape Cod Canal
on Wednesday, the twenty-ninth of July
Nineteen hundred and fourteen

R.S.V.P.
Forty-three Exchange Place
New York

August Belmont and the directors of the Cape Cod Construction Company sent out hundreds of formal invitations for the opening of the canal. This particular invitation was addressed to Derke Mulder, captain of the dredge *Federal*, at Sandwich.

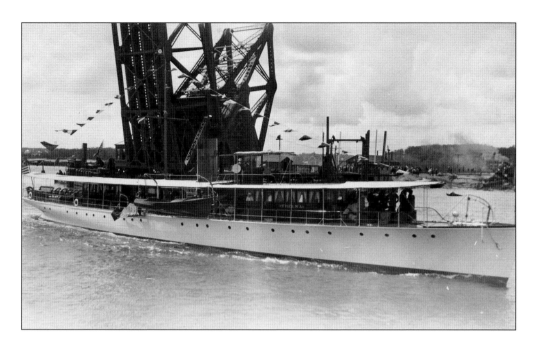

The commercial nature of the Cape Cod Canal was highlighted by the prominent place given in the procession to the seven yachts owned by the board of directors and investors. The *Thelma* (above) was the large yacht owned by Morton F. Plant, founder of the Plant system of railroads, one of the directors of August Belmont's Interborough Rapid Transit Company and a major investor in the Cape Cod Construction Company. The steam yachts *Linta, Alice, Sultana,* and *Oneida* were owned, respectively, by Walther Luttgen, F.D. Underwood, Mary Harriman, and E.C. Benedict. (Below, photograph by Fred C. Small.)

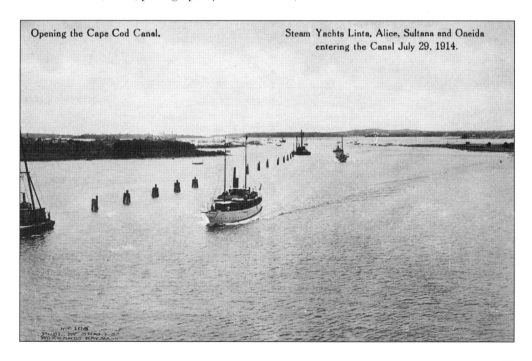

Opening the Cape Cod Canal.   Steam Yachts Linta, Alice, Sultana and Oneida entering the Canal July 29, 1914.

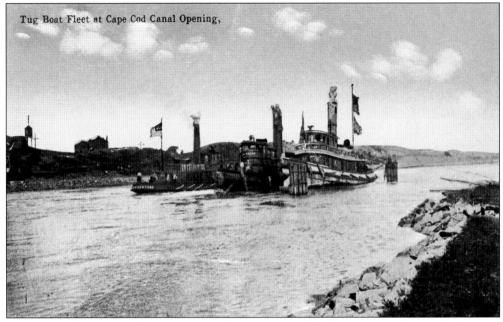

Tug Boat Fleet at Cape Cod Canal Opening,

A fleet of tugboats also took part in the parade, their owners likely glad for the increase in business that the canal would bring.

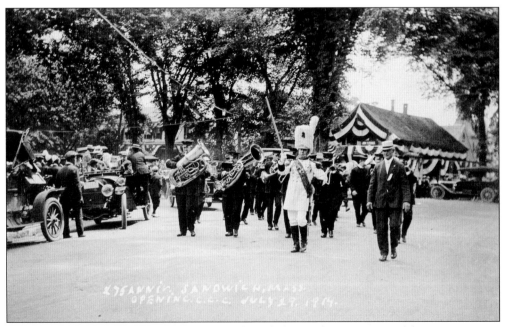

The opening of the canal was timed to coincide with the 275th anniversary of the incorporation of Sandwich, which included a parade with 50 floats and a gathering of 5,000 spectators. The band played "Hail to the Chief," and the chair of the reception committee presented a silver ceremonial loving cup to August Belmont.

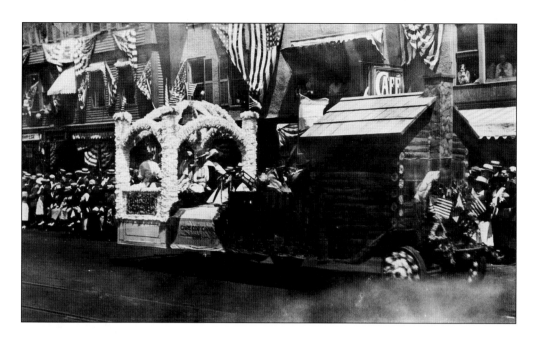

The floats in the Sandwich parade, like this one featuring both the Aptucxet Trading Post and the Cape Cod Canal, celebrated the town's past and future. A group of mounted officers also took part. In a speech at Town Neck, August Belmont tied his lineage through the Perry family to one of Sandwich's founders. He further pleased his audience by saying, "The Cape Cod Canal had its origins in Sandwich."

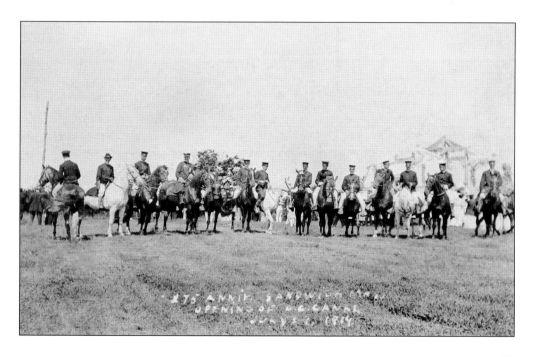

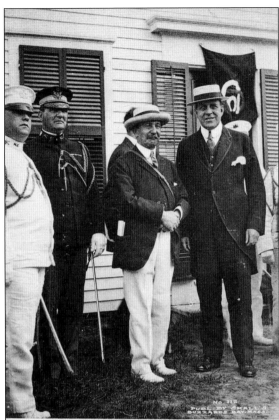

Opening the Cape Cod Canal.   Gov. Walsh and August Belmont.
July 29, 1914.

At left, Gov. David I. Walsh of Massachusetts (right) poses with August Belmont (center) and two unidentified military officers at the opening ceremonies for the Cape Cod Canal. Walsh and Belmont addressed the crowds first in Sandwich and afterwards in Bourne. Below, Walsh speaks to the large crowd gathered under a tent in Bourne for the opening ceremonies. Walsh praised Belmont's vision and perseverance as well as the town, the canal, and the potential for growth that they all shared. (Both, photograph by Fred C. Small.)

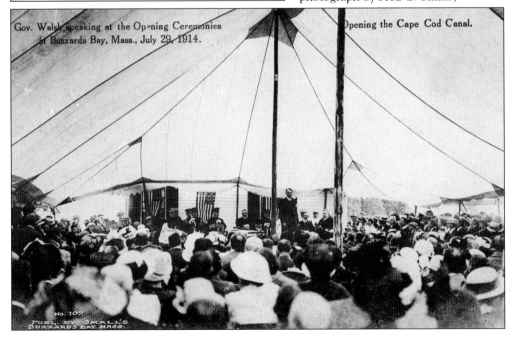

Gov. Walsh speaking at the Opening Ceremonies at Buzzards Bay, Mass., July 29, 1914.

Opening the Cape Cod Canal.

Bourne also had another celebration planned to coincide with the opening of the canal: the dedication of a new civic complex. The new Bourne Town Hall and Soldiers' and Sailors' Monument, both designed by architect James Purdon of Boston, were substantial Classical Revival additions, marking Bourne's new civic aspirations. Bourne sited them along the street leading to the new Bourne Bridge. (Both, photograph by Fred C. Small.)

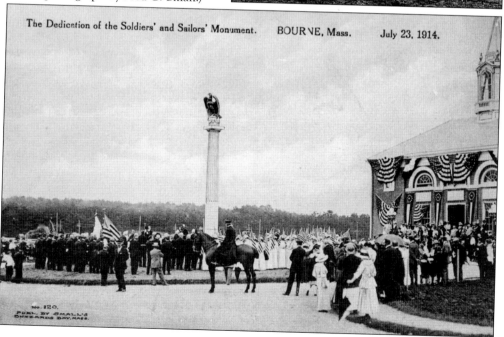

The Dedication of the Soldiers' and Sailors' Monument.   BOURNE, Mass.   July 23, 1914.

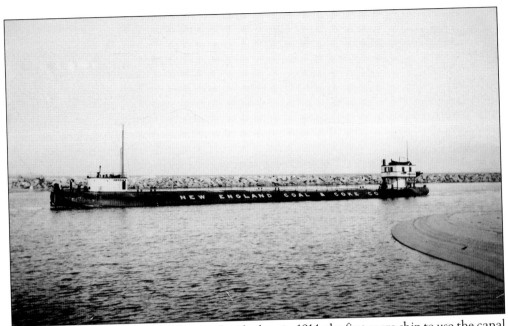

Although the grand opening of the canal took place in 1914, the first cargo ship to use the canal was this barge, the *Cassie*, a whaleback owned by New England Coal & Coke Company. On December 14, 1910, loaded with 2,000 tons of coal, it entered the Sandwich end of the canal, towed by the tugboat *Mary Arnold*. The canal provided a safe winter port along Sandwich's treacherous Cape Cod Bay shore.

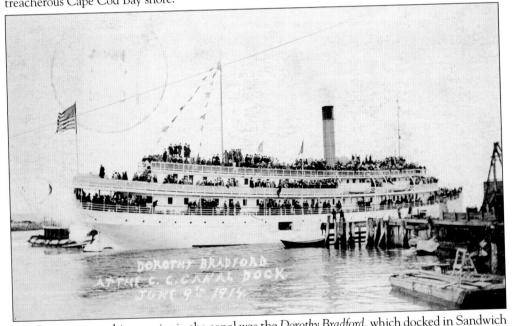

The first passenger ship to arrive in the canal was the *Dorothy Bradford*, which docked in Sandwich on June 9, 1914, more than a month before the grand opening. The passengers were members of the Boston Chamber of Commerce, civil engineers, and faculty and students from the Massachusetts Institute of Technology, curious to see the latest in canal technology. Half of the passengers got seasick on the way, though, and returned to Boston by train.

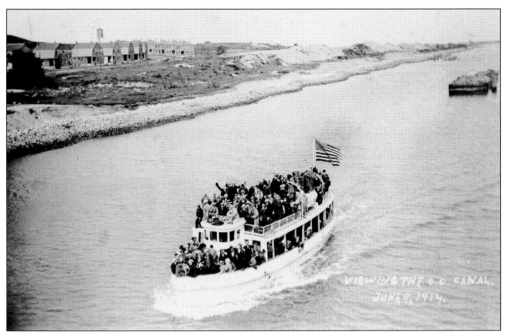

Some of the more adventurous of the *Dorothy Bradford* passengers transferred to this smaller boat and sailed as far as the Sagamore Bridge and the Keith Car Works. Writing to her friend Lulu Padelford in Whitman, Massachusetts, the author of this card wrote, "Oh! What a jolly crowd!"

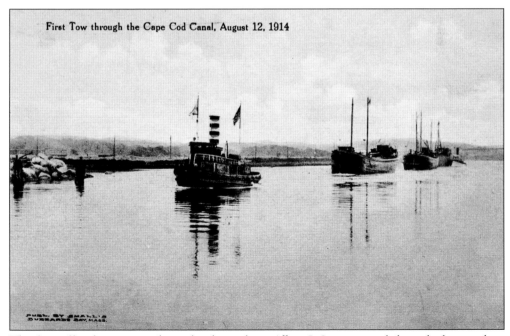

First Tow through the Cape Cod Canal, August 12, 1914

The first official commercial tow, by the tugboat *Albert J. Stone*, passed through the canal on August 12, 1914, two weeks after the grand opening. Behind it are three coal barges owned by the Erie Railroad: *Marion*, *Binghamton*, and *Pittston*.

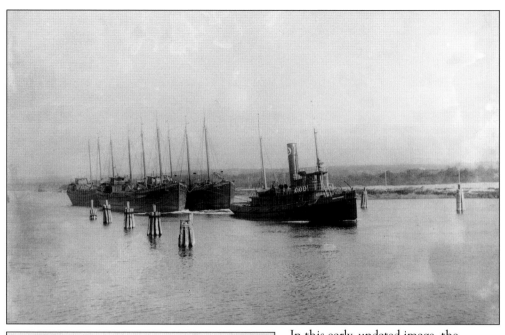

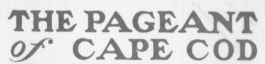

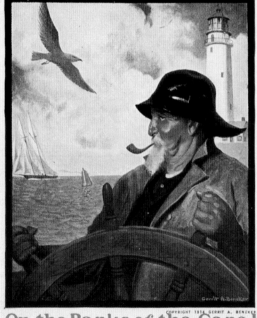

On the Banks of the Canal

LEAVE THE TRAIN AT BOURNE STATION

August 15 · 17 · 18 · 19 at 3 P.M

In this early, undated image, the tugboat *Honeybrook* tows a cluster of boats through the canal for the Lehigh and Wilkes Barre Coal Company. These boats were empty. The Cape Cod Construction Company had been able to dig only to a depth of 15 feet, which limited the types and sizes of boats that could use the canal that first year. Not until 1916 did it complete the canal to a minimum depth of 25 feet and bottom width of 100 feet, as originally planned.

The townspeople of Bourne staged an elaborate *Pageant of Cape Cod* alongside the canal in August 1914. Artist Gerrit A. Beneker asked a Provincetown sea captain, celebrated for saving a crew of seven from a shipwreck, to pose for this poster.

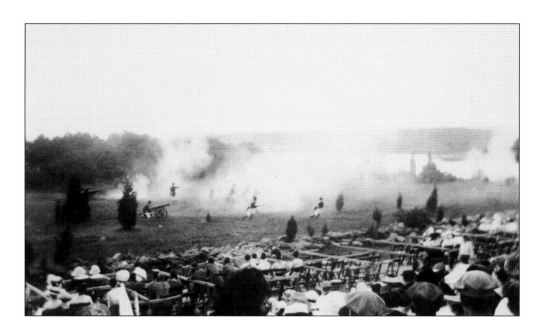

The Pageant of Cape Cod included more than a dozen vignettes, such as the "Bombardment of Falmouth" (above) and the unidentified scene below, viewed by spectators from the Bourne Bridge. Performers from a dozen nearby communities joined together to present the pageant, which combined music, poetry, historical reenactments, and interpretive dance. The penultimate scene, "The New Cape," included discussions of scientific agriculture, egg circles, forest fire prevention, and "manliness" training. These pageants were popular forms of public entertainment in the early decades of 20th century before the advent of radio.

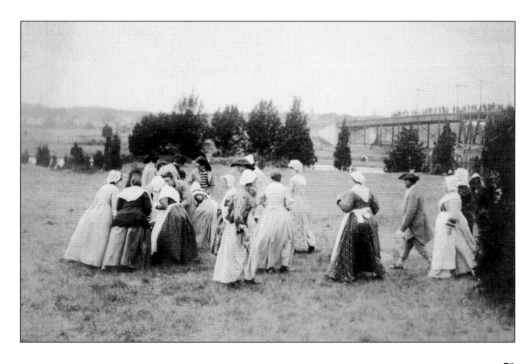

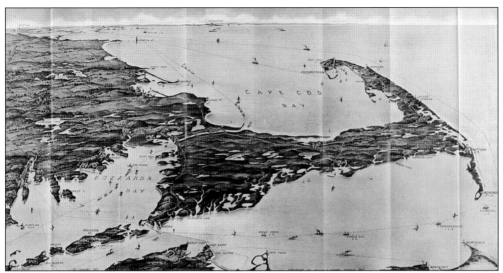

This 1915 bird's-eye view of Cape Cod shows how dramatically the newly opened Cape Cod Canal shortened the water connections between Boston and New York. (Map by Albert E. Downs for New England News.)

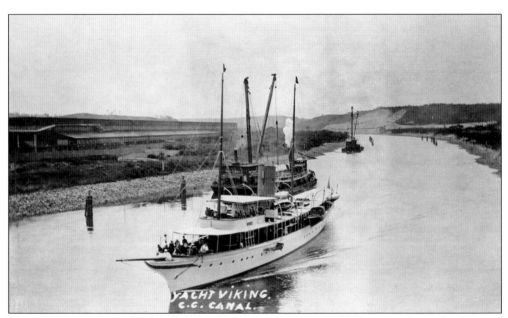

The yacht *Viking* passes by the Keith Car Works near Sagamore. Yachting guides and magazines of the late 1910s celebrated the experience of navigating the canal.

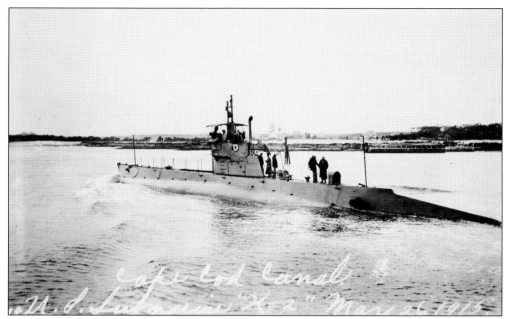

On May 26, 1915, the crew of the US submarine X2 came up on deck to enjoy the view while crossing through the Cape Cod Canal.

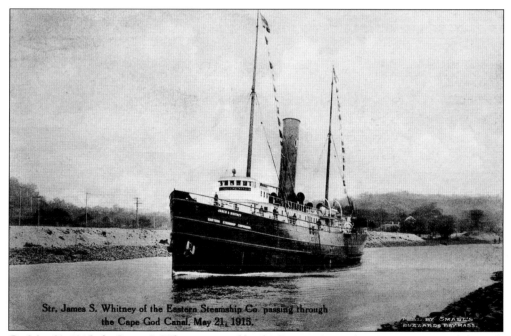

On May 21, 1915, the *James S. Whitney*, owned by the Eastern Steamship Company, passed through the Cape Cod Canal. Charles Wyman Morse formed the company in 1901 by merging several New England steamship lines. Struggling to compete with J.P. Morgan's Fall River Line, Eastern became the first steamship company to use the Cape Cod Canal on a regular basis. (Photograph by Fred C. Small.)

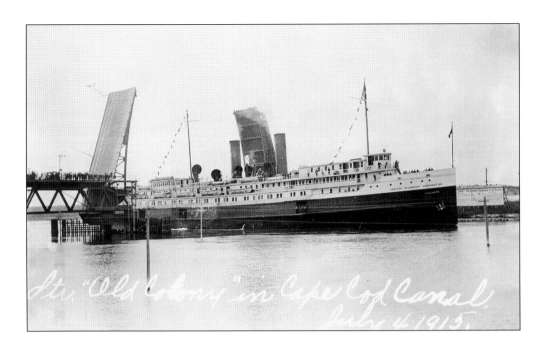

Str. "Old Colony" in Cape Cod Canal, July 4, 1915.

On July 4, 1915, the steamer *Old Colony* entered the Cape Cod Canal on a test cruise, and photographers were ready. Crowds lined up to watch it pass through the Bourne Bridge (above), while Fred Small set up his camera at one of his favorite vantage points, the same place where he had photographed Foley's Dyke. In 1916, the Eastern Steamship Company agreed to use the Cape Cod Canal exclusively for all of its Boston–New York runs for a flat toll rate of $125 per passage. (Below, photograph by Fred C. Small.)

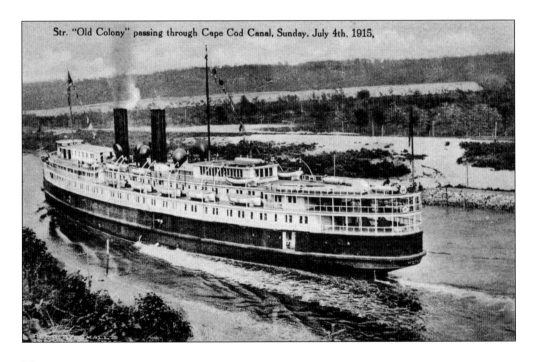

Str. "Old Colony" passing through Cape Cod Canal, Sunday, July 4th, 1915.

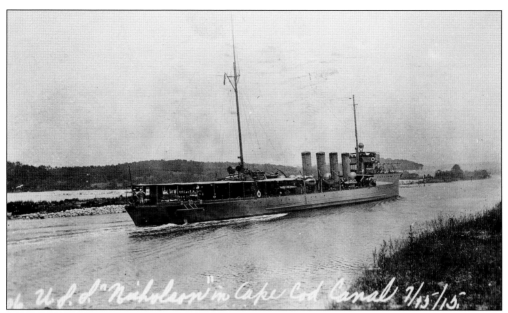

On July 15, 1915, the USS *Nicholson* crossed through the Cape Cod Canal. By 1915, the canal channel had been deepened to 18–20 feet.

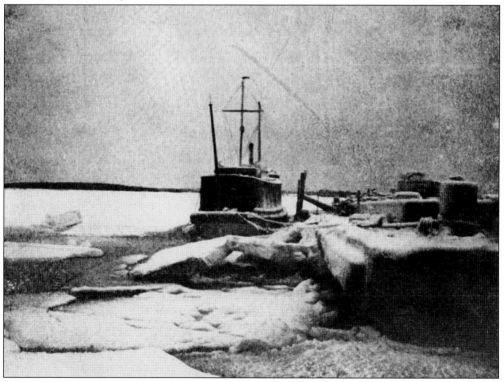

In 1917, the launch *Helen May* is shown almost stranded among large ice blocks at Monument Beach Pier, near the western entrance to the Cape Cod Canal. Operated by the Vineyard Haven branch of the Boston Seaman's Friend Society, the *Helen May* had been serving sailors on ships and bringing them to the Martha's Vineyard's Bethel Chapel for services since 1893.

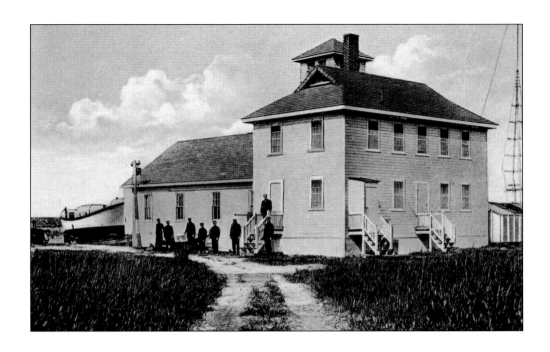

The US Coast Guard built this full-time station (above) in Sandwich in 1917 to handle calls along the new Cape Cod Canal. Located on the south side of the canal entrance, this station was relatively small and struggled to effectively deal with rumrunners during Prohibition. In 1935, the Coast Guard demolished both the station and the boathouse for the expansion of the canal and built a new station farther back from the bank. Coast Guard members and their mascot line up for a portrait below.

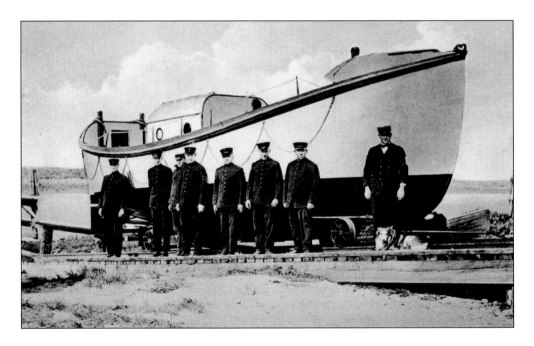

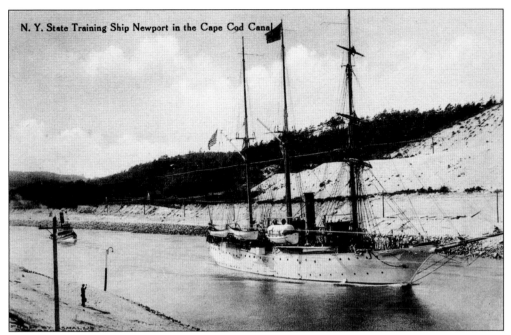

On September 19, 1914, the USS *Newport,* a nautical school ship operated by the State of New York, passed through the Cape Cod Canal. (Photograph by Fred C. Small.)

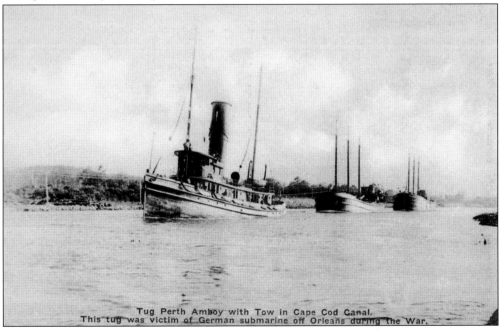

The little tugboat *Perth Amboy* ended the days of the Cape Cod Canal operating as a private commercial enterprise. Shown here in a Fred C. Small photograph, the *Perth Amboy* was a frequent visitor to the canal. On July 21, 1918, the *Perth Amboy* was hauling a string of barges off Orleans when the German submarine *U-156* shelled them, sinking the barges and setting the tugboat ablaze. On July 22, Pres. Woodrow Wilson signed an order placing control of the canal with the Railroad Administration, under the Department of War. (Photograph by Fred C. Small.)

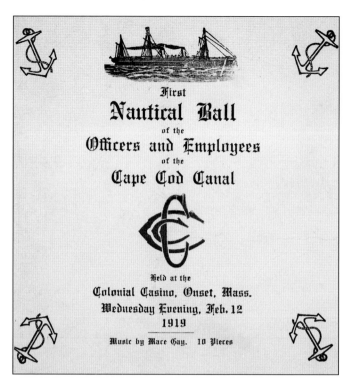

First
Nautical Ball
of the
Officers and Employees
of the
Cape Cod Canal

Held at the
Colonial Casino, Onset, Mass.
Wednesday Evening, Feb. 12
1919

Music by Mace Gay.   10 Pieces

On February 12, 1919, the officers and civilian employees of the Cape Cod Canal held a Nautical Ball. Its formal program began with a Grand March "to all hands, and the ship's cook!" The dances were waltzes, one-steps, two-steps, and foxtrots, dedicated variously to the pilots, bridge boys, engineers, boatmen, signalmen, tugboat crews, dispatchers, and the Bourne District nurse. Each dance had a title such as "Ship Ahoy," "Port Your Helm," "Breakers Ahead," or "Wing's Neck Light on Starboard Bow." The invited guests included Capt. and Mrs. H.L. Colbeth and Capt. Arthur Crowley.

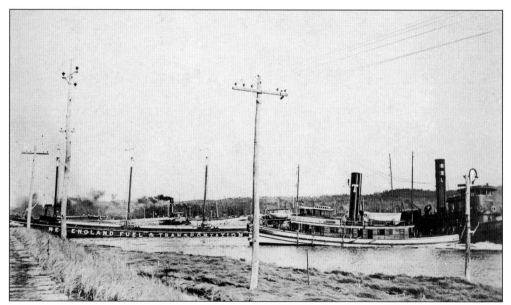

In Bourne on March 25, 1919, the barge *Helen* (left, marked "New England Fuel and Transportation") broke its tow and hit the bank. The tugboats successfully maneuvered her back into the channel again. But other cases were more complicated; when the collier *Bayport* crashed into the bank in 1916, it blocked the canal for three months and had to be dynamited.

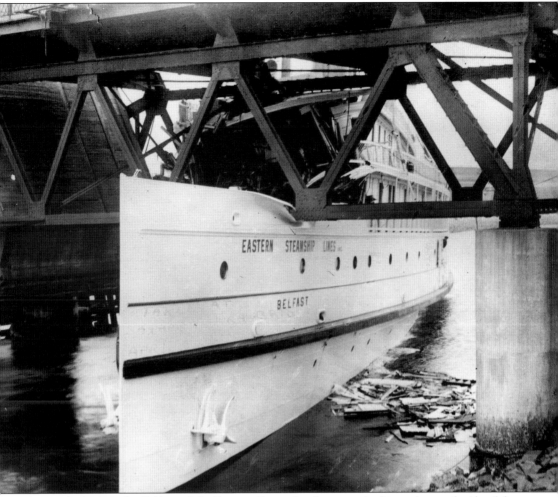

On April 16, 1919, the *Belfast*, of the Eastern Steamship Line, crashed into the north side of the Sagamore Bridge. Two passengers and a crew member sustained injuries. The *Belfast* was removed and rerouted after a day. Given the volume of traffic in the Cape Cod Canal, these accidents might be expected. But the cumulative bad publicity dissuaded many users from patronizing the canal. (Photograph by Fred C. Small; courtesy of Bourne Historical Society.)

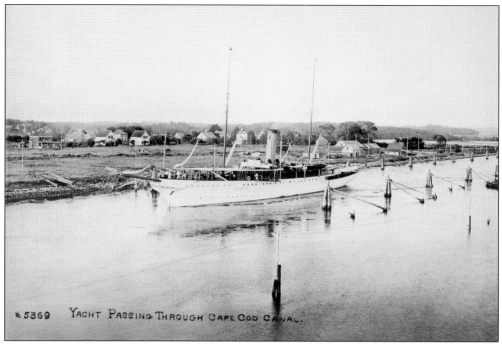

This photograph of a yacht passing through the Cape Cod Canal plays up the picturesque character of the journey, with views of open fields, distant houses, and tall trees. (Photograph by New England News.)

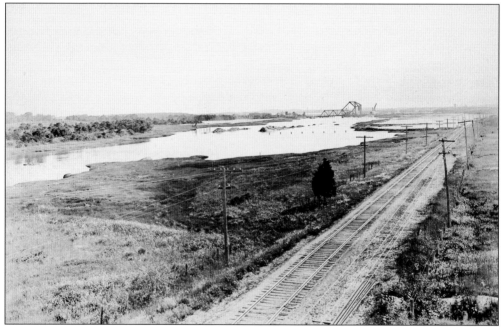

The Cape Cod Canal is deserted in this 1920 view from the north bank of the canal, looking west towards Bourne. But the Buzzards Bay Railroad Bridge in the far background is one of several signs that change has come to the placid tidal waters of the Monument River. (Photograph by Samuel N. Wood.)

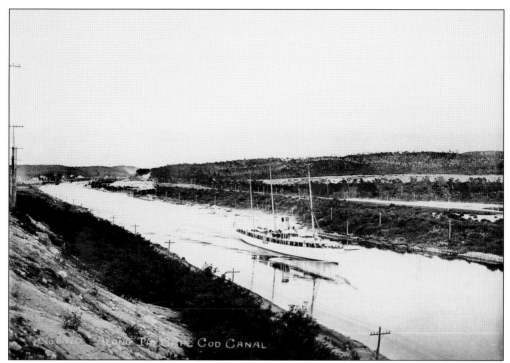

Because of their closeness to the roadway and high elevation, certain vantage points attracted many photographers. The cover photograph of this book, for example, shows the dredge *Governor Warfield* opening up the canal, from this same spot, a decade earlier. (Photograph by New England News.)

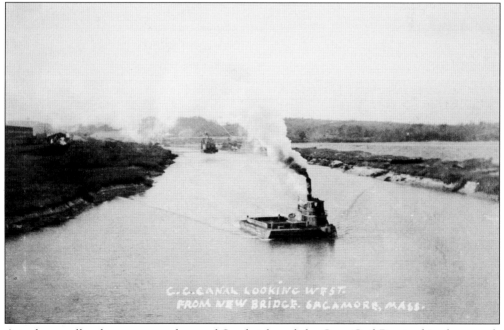

A tugboat pulls a barge eastward toward Sandwich and the Cape Cod Bay in this photograph taken from the Sagamore Bridge shortly after its completion.

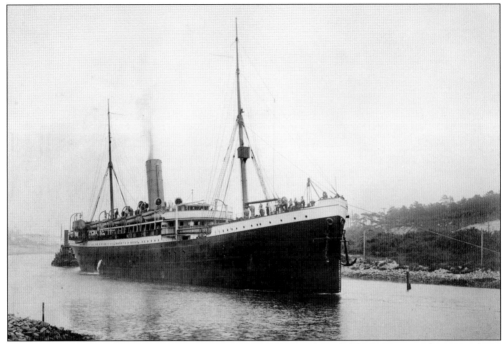

The *Willehad* is shown passing through the Cape Cod Canal, probably in 1917. Built in Hamburg in 1894, the *Willehad* was a passenger liner and one of several German ships detained at Boston Harbor in 1914 at the beginning of the European conflict. The US government remained neutral until 1917, when it seized the German ships. The US Navy likely used the *Willehad* as a troop transport, which was the fate of its twin, the *Wittekind*. (Photograph by Fred C. Small; courtesy of Bourne Historical Society.)

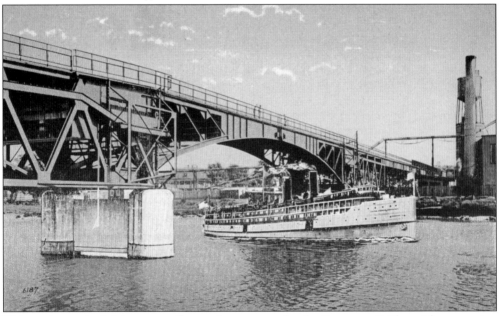

This moderate-sized ship was small enough to pass under the Sagamore Bridge without causing the draw to be raised.

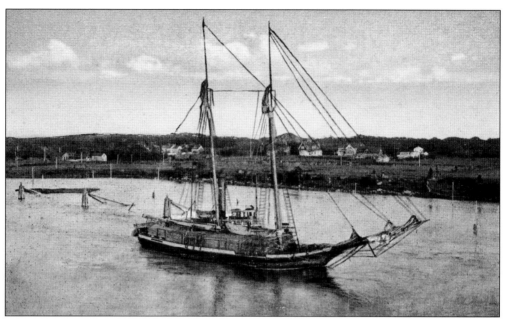

A two-masted schooner passes through the Cape Cod Canal near Bourne.

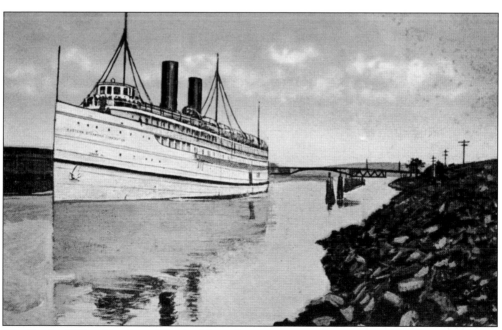

The *Bunker Hill* and its sister ship, the *Massachusetts*, were regular visitors to the Cape Cod Canal as part of the fleet of coastal passenger steamers operated by the Eastern Steamship Line. Both were built in 1907 in Philadelphia and renovated in 1912 for a Boston to New York route. After trial runs in 1915, they regularly passed through the canal in 1916.

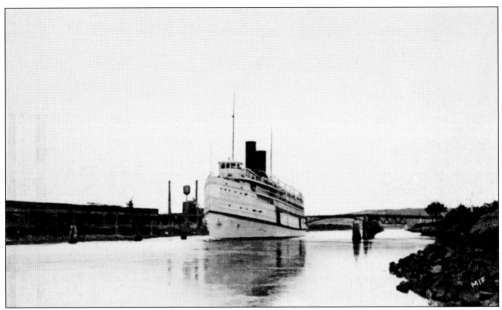

In 1917, the US Navy acquired the *Bunker Hill* and the *Massachusetts*, ending this early chapter in coastal cruising. At the Boston Navy Yard, the Navy converted them into minelayers. The *Bunker Hill* was renamed the USS *Aroostook*, while the *Massachusetts* became the USS *Shawmut*. Each laid thousands of mines in the North Sea to deter German U-boats. After the war, they were converted again, into seaplane tenders. The *Aroostook* went idle and was scrapped in 1947. But the *Massachusetts/Shawmut* became the USS *Oglala* in 1928. Sunk during the Pearl Harbor, Hawaii, air attack in 1941, it was salvaged and refloated, serving other purposes until scrapped in 1965.

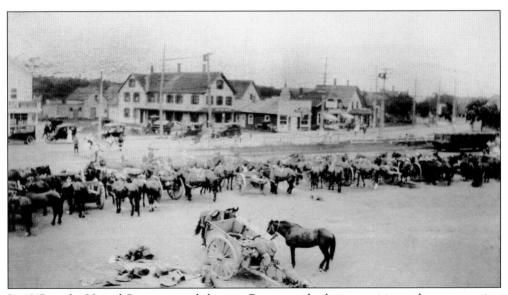

In 1917, as the United States entered the war, Bourne and other port cities and transportation hubs became mustering centers for the war. This image of Bourne preparing for war activity likely dates to the early days of United States involvement in 1917.

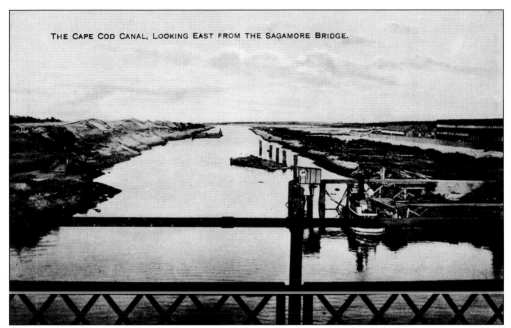

THE CAPE COD CANAL, LOOKING EAST FROM THE SAGAMORE BRIDGE.

A single tugboat waits in the canal east of the Sagamore Bridge. This postcard image was published by H.A. Dickerman and Son of Taunton; however, it was printed in Germany because German companies had perfected high-quality, inexpensive color lithography. With the advent of the world war, many American companies switched to printing their own postcards.

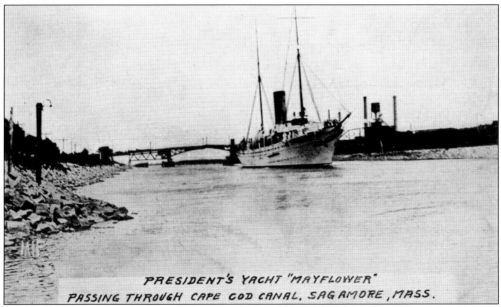

PRESIDENT'S YACHT "MAYFLOWER"
PASSING THROUGH CAPE COD CANAL, SAGAMORE, MASS.

On July 31, 1921, Pres. Warren G. Harding and his wife anchored the presidential yacht, the USS *Mayflower*, in Buzzards Bay off the Wings Neck lighthouse for the night. Early the next morning, they traveled through the Cape Cod Canal on their way to Plymouth, Massachusetts, to take part in the Pilgrim tercentenary observances. (Photograph by Manuel I. Ferreira.)

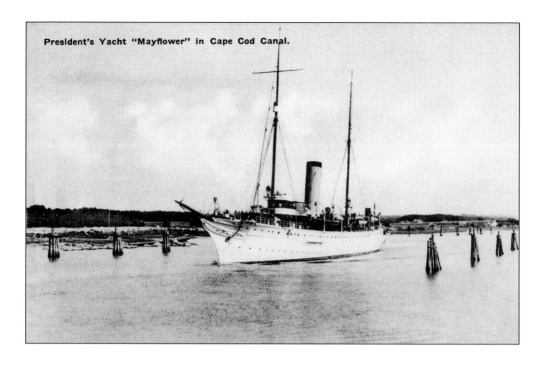

President's Yacht "Mayflower" in Cape Cod Canal.

Thousands of well-wishers greeted President Harding along the banks of the canal; the visit was seen by several commentators to symbolize that the government would permanently assume control of the canal. The USS *Mayflower* was a steam yacht built in 1896 in Scotland, purchased by the US Navy from the estate of its first owner in 1898 for service in the Spanish-American War. It served as the presidential yacht from 1905 to 1929, most prominently as a meeting place for the delegations signing the peace treaty ending the Russo-Japanese War in 1905. Pres. Herbert Hoover got rid of the yacht after assuming office. Below, a boy is strategically posed in front of the passing yacht. (Above, photograph by Fred C. Small.)

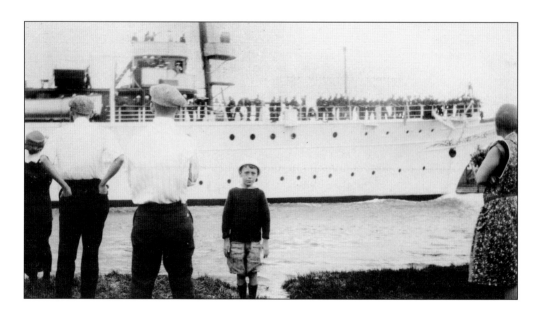

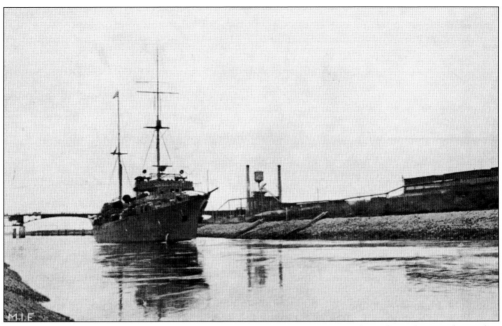

Under government control, military traffic in the canal increased, with such vessels as this submarine tender frequenting the canal. (Photograph by Manuel I. Ferreira.)

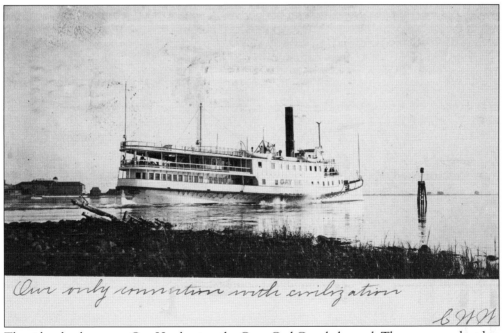

The side-wheel steamer *Gay Head* enters the Cape Cod Canal channel. The correspondent has written under the image, "Our only connection with civilization." Built in 1891 for the New Bedford, Martha's Vineyard, and Nantucket Steamboat Company, the steamer was named for the Massachusetts town Gay Head, now known as Aquinnah. The steamer operated until 1924.

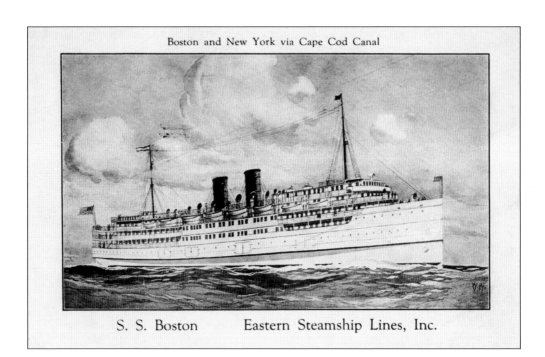

Boston and New York via Cape Cod Canal

S. S. Boston   Eastern Steamship Lines, Inc.

After the World War I, the Eastern Steamship Line reinvested in ships, replacing its ragtag fleet with two new boats purposely built for the Boston to New York trade: the SS *Boston* and the SS *New York*. Launched in 1922, they were described as "steel, oil-burning, geared turbine-driven, twin-screw, express steamers" that each carried 900 passengers. The fare for the half-day trip was between $5.50 and $6.50. The cruise brochure featured an inset map of the Cape Cod Canal and the slogan "Sheltered All the Way! Through Massachusetts Bay—Cape Cod Canal—Buzzards Bay—Long Island Sound."

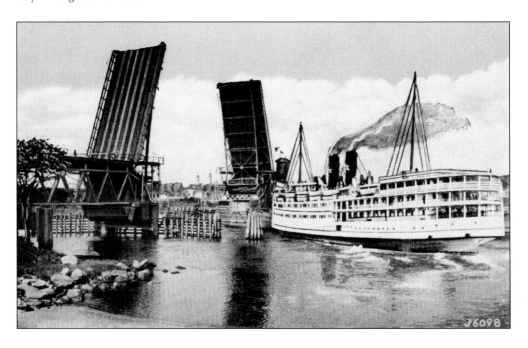

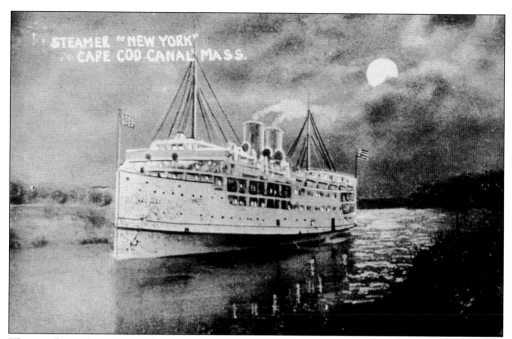

The numbers of passengers through the canal climbed steadily throughout the 1920s, but the total number of ships and gross tonnage of shipping held steady or declined. The public and military advantages of the Cape Cod Canal were clear, but some critics counseled against the government acquiring the canal. Arguing that the canal was too small and shallow, a columnist for the *Nation* labeled it "Wall Street's White Elephant."

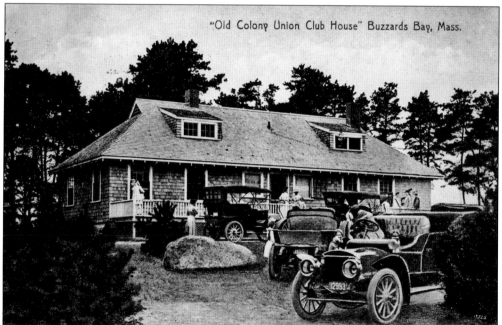

The Old Colony Union Club House opened in 1911, on a site overlooking Bourne Pond. It was primarily a tearoom that sold handicrafts made by students at the Old Colony Union Industrial School. (Photograph by Fred C. Small.)

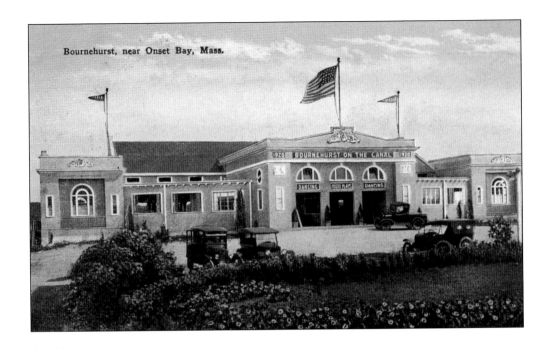

Bournehurst, near Onset Bay, Mass.

One of the most popular gathering spots of the 1920s was Bournehurst on the Canal, a huge entertainment complex in Bourne. It hosted fine dinners, motion pictures, and live music by bandleaders such as Duke Ellington, Guy Lombardo, and Rudy Vallee.

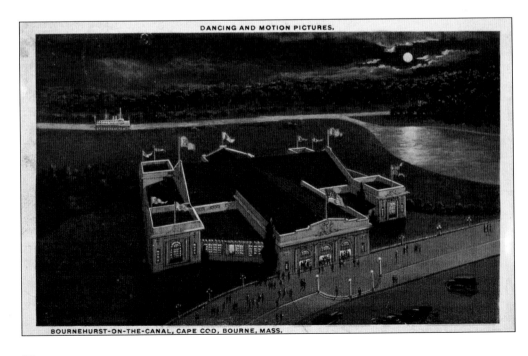

DANCING AND MOTION PICTURES.

BOURNEHURST-ON-THE-CANAL, CAPE COD, BOURNE, MASS.

Four

LEISURE
A PUBLIC CANAL

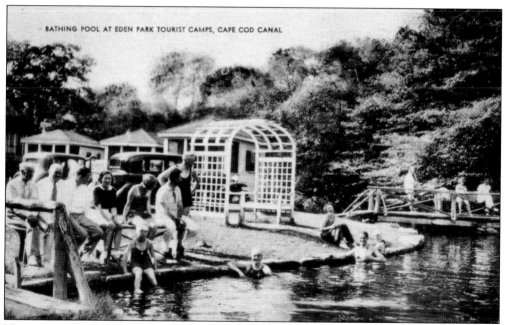

BATHING POOL AT EDEN PARK TOURIST CAMPS, CAPE COD CANAL

Vacationers enjoy a brief swim at the bathing pool at the Eden Park Tourist Camps in Bournedale in 1938. The days of the Cape Cod Canal as a commercial venture—a private toll canal—were relatively brief as well, from its opening in 1914 until the transfer of ownership to the federal government in March 1928. If one subtracts the war years—1918 to 1920, when the canal was under the direct control of the Railroad Administration—then its commercial lifespan was less than a dozen years. But starting in 1928, the new owners would transform the Cape Cod Canal, building new bridges and a much deeper, wider, and straighter canal. The changes would both greatly increase the commercial traffic through the canal and renew the canal's role as a center for leisure and recreation.

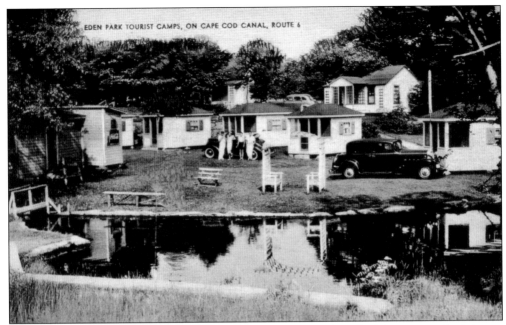

Not only was Eden Park directly on the canal, but it appears to have had its own set of miniature canals and bridges. Tourist camps were popular from the 1930s through the 1950s. They replaced the old railroad hotels near depots with new, more individualized lodging experiences, catering to the freedom and mobility the automobile gave the rising middle class. The camps also marketed smartly with free postcards. The writers of both this postcard and the Eden Park postcard on the previous page testified that they had "stayed here last night."

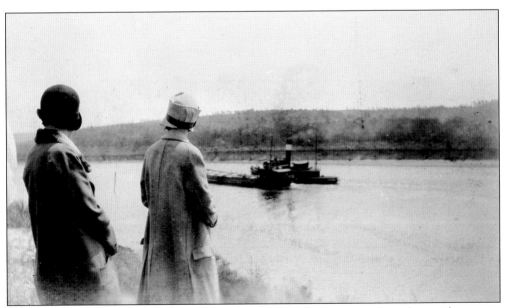

The automobile also provided new mobility and freedom for women, such as these sightseers.

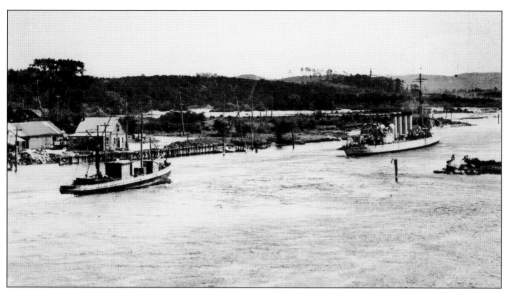

A US Navy destroyer (right) tows the Canadian *Marienendole*, detained as a rumrunner, through the Cape Cod Canal in July 1929. In effect from 1920 to 1933, Prohibition banned the legal sale of alcohol in the United States, thereby spurring its illegal trafficking. According to newspaper reports, "Dry men say she has loaded many a cargo."

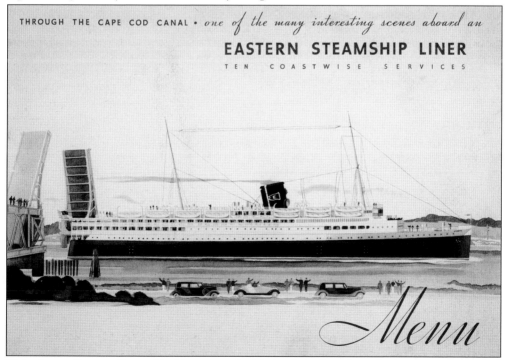

This elegant Eastern Steamship Liner menu highlighted the fun of watching and being watched on the large "coastwise" passenger ships: "Through the Cape Cod Canal—one of the many interesting scenes." The steamship line was a big backer of plans to expand the canal since the *Acadia*, the boat seen here, was too large to navigate the canal in all seasons. But World War II and the automobile brought an end to the coastal steamers by 1941.

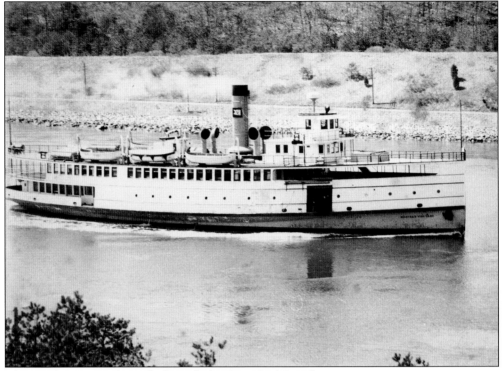

The *Martha's Vineyard* travels through the Cape Cod Canal.

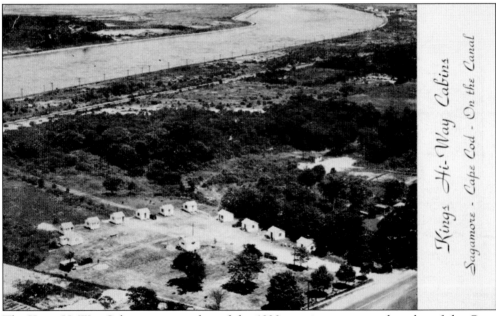

The Kings Hi-Way Cabins were another of the 1930s tourist camps on the edge of the Cape Cod Canal (seen in the upper left). During this time, Bourne began to get a reputation as an intermediate stop on the edge of Cape Cod, the kind of place where one might spend the night before driving on to Hyannis or Provincetown. These cabins were a forerunner of the motor hotel, or motel.

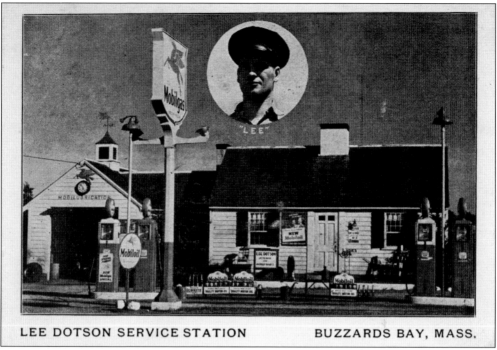

LEE DOTSON SERVICE STATION   BUZZARDS BAY, MASS.

The Lee Dotson Service Station in Buzzards Bay, shown here around 1940.

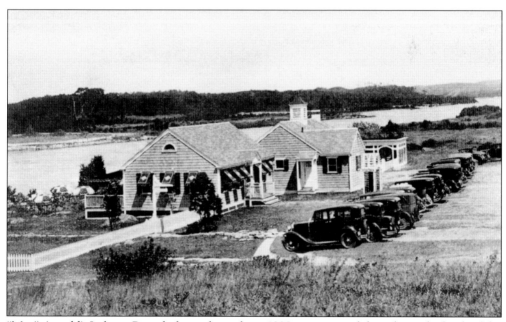

"Mac" Arnold's Lobster Pound, shown here about 1928, was situated directly on the bank of the canal near the Bourne Bridge. According to a 1936 menu, the secret to freshness was a lobster tank immersed in the canal itself: "You will find 'Mac' Arnold's lobsters especially enjoyable, as they are taken from the cold water of the canal and immediately cooked, retaining their tender freshness and delicious flavor."

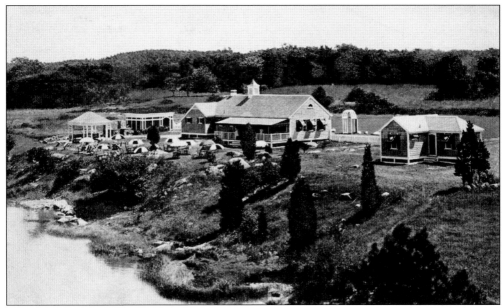

This view shows "Mac" Arnold's Lobster Pound from the vantage point of a ship on the Cape Cod Canal. In 1935, Arnold served cocktails and catered to afternoon bridge (the card game) parties. A 1937 menu featured the restaurant's "Canal Special," which included a hot boiled lobster with steamed clams, clam broth, Saratoga chips, rolls, drawn butter, pickles, tea or coffee, and sherbet or ice cream, all for $1.50.

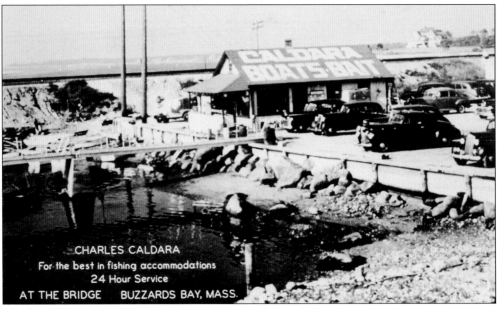

Charles Caldara ran a fishing expedition service in Buzzards Bay, shown in this photograph from about 1940. Fishing and sightseeing cruises became an important tourist draw in Bourne.

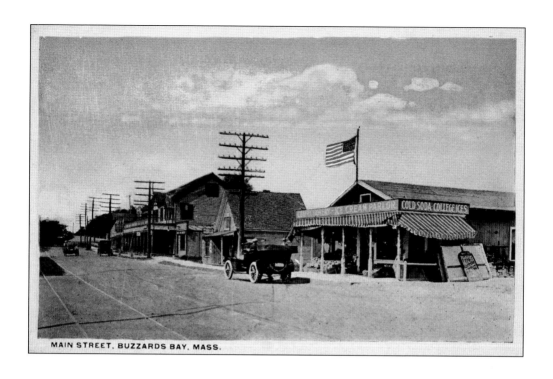

MAIN STREET, BUZZARDS BAY, MASS.

The photographs on this page and the next show the evolution of the village of Buzzards Bay, on the mainland side of the canal, during the first half of the 20th century, as it became the transportation and tourism hub of the town of Bourne and the jumping-off point for exploring the canal and Cape Cod. The above image is a postcard view of the business strip in the late 1910s; below is a snapshot from the late 1920s.

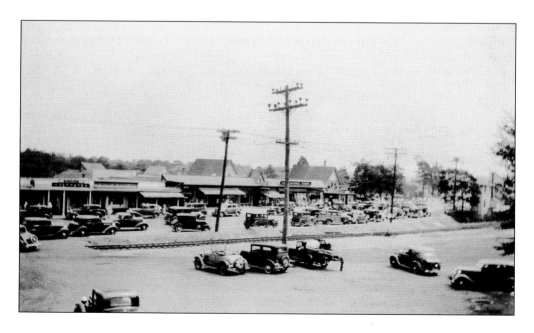

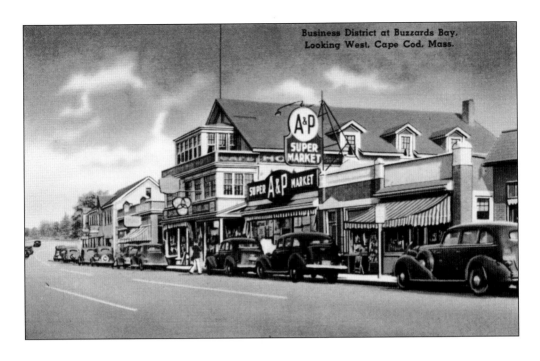

These postcard views show the Buzzards Bay business district about 1937 (above) and in 1946 (below). They focus on the strip of business buildings facing the canal and the ample parking for tourists. (Below, photograph by Curt Teich and Company.)

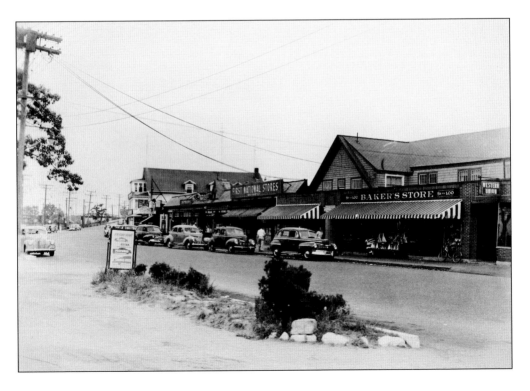

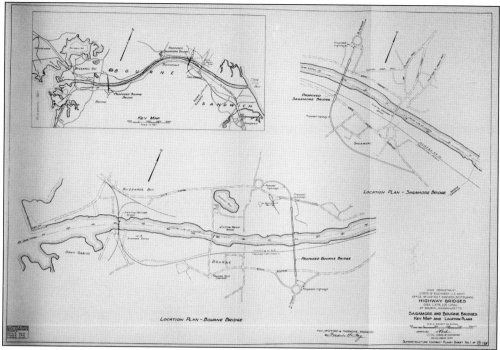

This 1933 map shows how the new Bourne and Sagamore Bridges would transform the landscape. The map also shows the cut-off courses of streets closed in the early 1910s when a previous set of highway and railroad bridges was removed. Particularly unfortunate was the way that the new bridges relegated the 1914 Bourne Town Hall to a side street. (Map by US Army Corps of Engineers.)

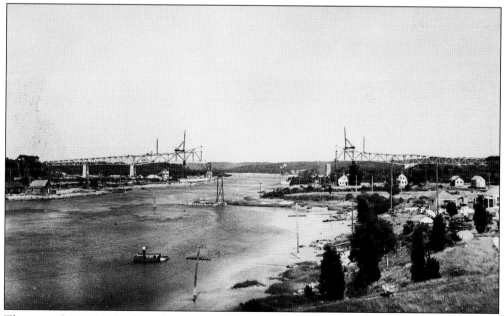

The next three images show the construction of the Bourne Bridge in 1933 and 1934. Federal ownership made possible the improvements to the canal and bridge system that its users had been seeking since the canal opened in 1914.

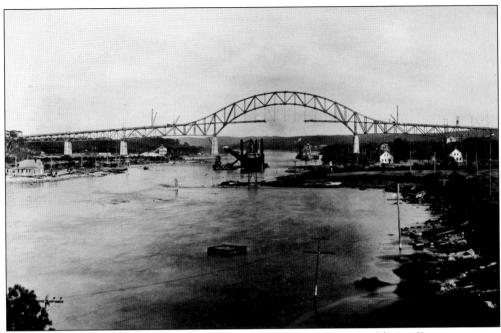

The Bourne Bridge nears completion in 1933–1934. Congress authorized $35 million to improve the Cape Cod Canal. Nearly $5 million of those funds went to three bridges: the Bourne and Sagamore highway bridges and the Buzzards Bay Railroad Bridge. Travelers today can be glad that initial plans for a single central bridge were successfully derailed by the inhabitants of Bourne and Sagamore. The traffic backups on a single bridge would be hard to imagine, and any bridge closures would completely cut off Cape Cod from the mainland. In the image above, the dredge *Governor Herrick*, so instrumental in bringing the canal to completion in 1913 and 1914, works to widen the canal channel.

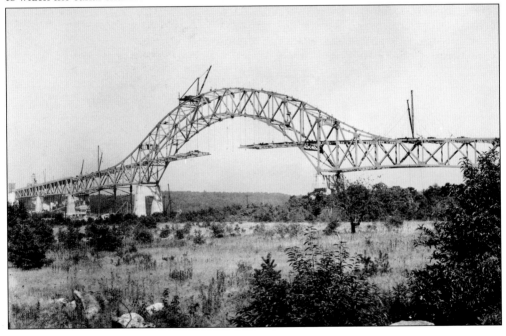

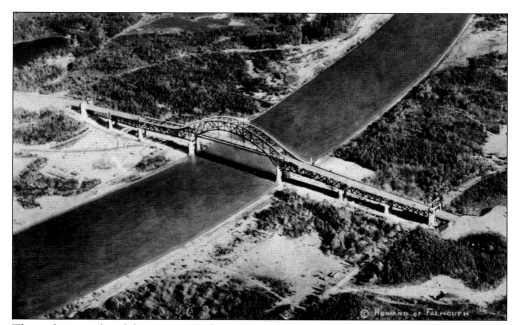

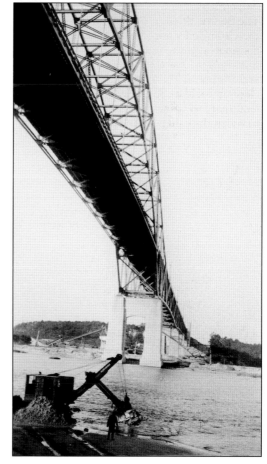

These photographs of the Bourne Bridge show excavations at the base of the new bridge in December 1934 (right) and the completed bridge from the air (above). Planners agreed that the new Cape Cod Canal bridges could not be drawbridges like the ones that they replaced because of the delays that would result to both canal and highway traffic. The two high-level highway bridges shared the same design, with a clearance of 135 feet above the canal's high water mark—the same clearance as the Brooklyn Bridge.

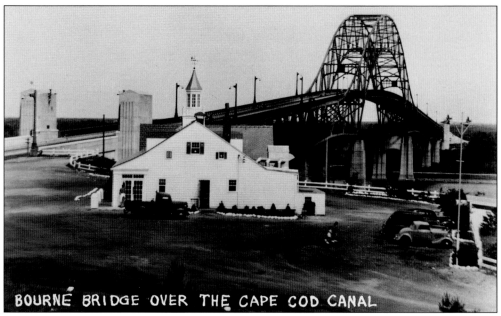

BOURNÉ BRIDGE OVER THE CAPE COD CANAL

Traffic rotaries were part of the early designs of both bridges on the Cape Cod Canal. This early view shows the Cape Cod side of the Bourne Bridge, with a Howard Johnson's Restaurant on the traffic rotary. The building later became a Bob's Big Boy and then an International House of Pancakes.

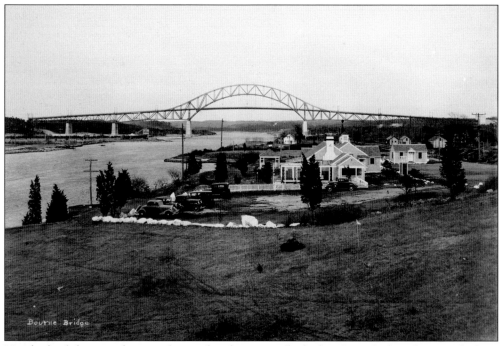

Bourne Bridge

Hundreds of photographers, professional and amateur, flocked to Cape Cod to photograph these impressive new bridges. This spot on the mainland side of the canal was probably the most photographed view in Bourne. The parking lot and low buildings belong to "Mac" Arnold's Lobster Pound.

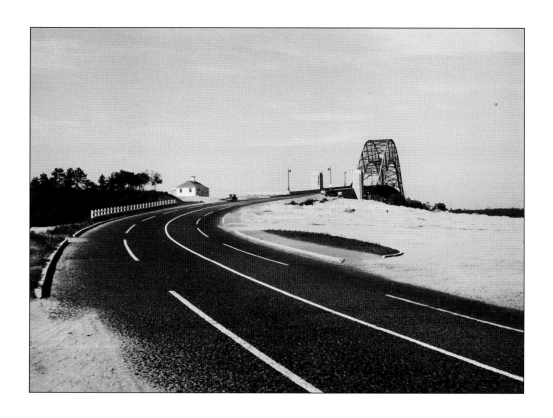

These views show the Bourne Bridge from the mainland side shortly after completion (above) and from several miles away (below), as two ships pass on the canal. One of the goals in widening the canals was to allow ships to travel safely in both directions at the same time. (Above, photograph by Curt Teich and Company.)

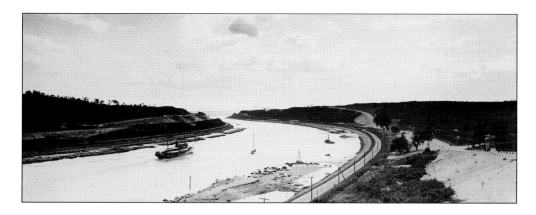

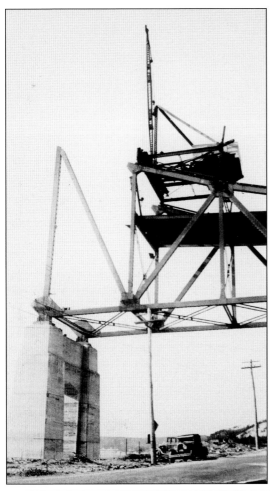

These two photographs show the Sagamore Bridge under construction in 1934. In the image at left, workers have completed the reinforced concrete piers on the north side of the bridge and are beginning to install the superstructure. Both the Bourne and Sagamore Bridges have steel trusses supporting a reinforced concrete floor 40 feet wide. Each has a central span that is 660 feet long.

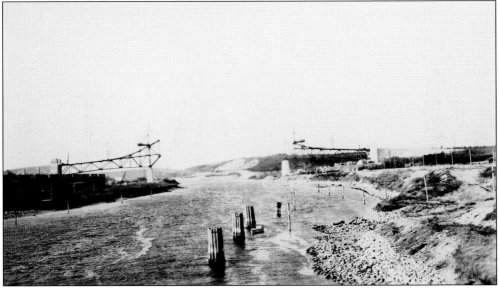

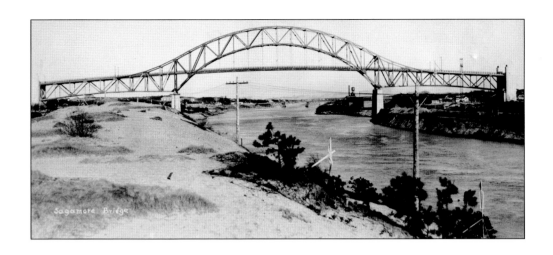

Completed in 1935, the Sagamore Bridge attracted photographers, just as the Bourne Bridge had. In the image below, taken in September 1937, a motorist poses at the entry to the Sagamore Bridge, below its name panel. The Boston firm of Fay, Spofford, and Thorndyke completed the engineering plans for the bridges. They hired the Boston architectural firm of Cram and Ferguson as architectural consultants. The bridges may seem far removed from the Gothic-style churches that Ralph Adams Cram is best known for, but his firm consulted on a wide variety of designs nationwide. The bridges won national prizes for their engineering and architecture.

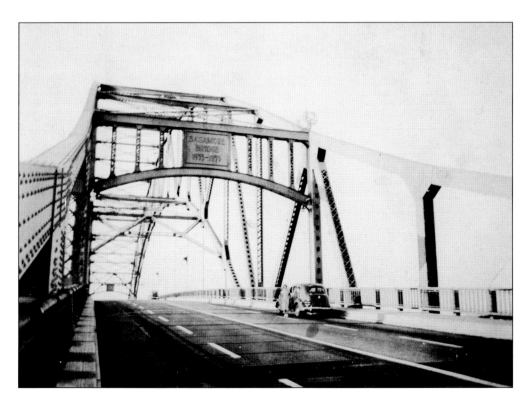

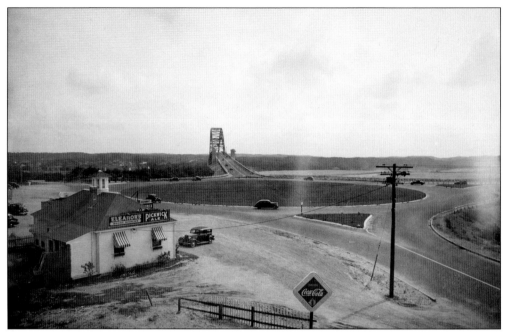

Eleanor's Restaurant, shown here advertising its shore dinners and Pickwick Ale, stood on the western approach rotary to the Sagamore Bridge. In the 1950s, the building was moved to Meeting House Road in Sagamore. It had a reputation as a neighborhood restaurant that specialized in home-baked pies.

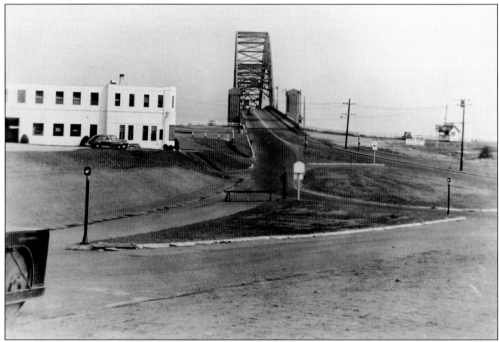

The entries to the canal bridges have been reconfigured many times, including the 2007 elimination of the western Sagamore rotary, which had previously confused out-of-state drivers and had become impractical as well as a bottleneck. (Photograph by Curt Teich and Company.)

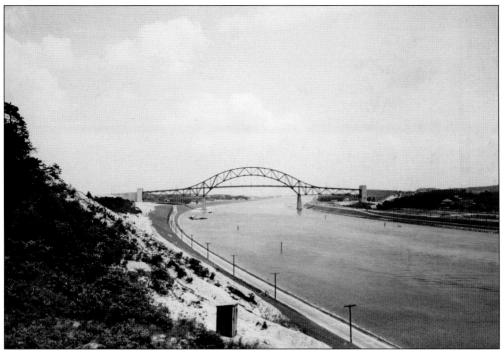

This photograph shows the Sagamore Bridge as completed in 1935. Once they finished the new bridges, the planners focused on the real work of widening the canal, beginning with demolishing the old bridges and removing their pilings from the canal.

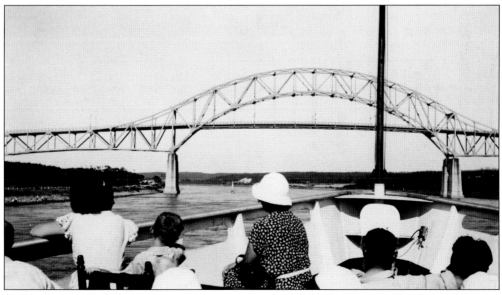

In this August 15, 1948, image, passengers enjoy a view of the Sagamore Bridge during a Sunday canal cruise on the *Liberty Belle*.

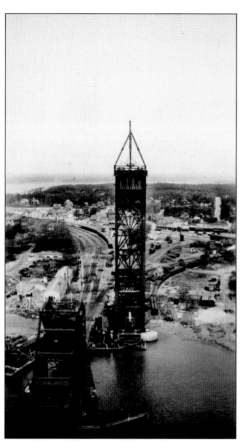

This 1935 view from the north tower of the canal's railroad bridge shows the south tower completed and waiting for the bridge itself to be installed. Directly to the left is the 1911 railroad bridge. Funded by the National Industrial Recovery Act of 1933, construction of the three bridges provided jobs for 700 or more workers. Administered through the Public Works Administration, these jobs were a welcome relief to many Massachusetts workers during the Great Depression.

A model poses in the middle of a bearings sheave and housing assembly for the Cape Cod Canal Railroad Bridge shortly before its installation in 1935. The unique nature of the railroad lift bridge led to numerous engineering innovations. The Torrington Company based the design of these innovative bearings on the specialized units used in heavy cranes in steel mills. Each bearing assembly weighs 9,000 pounds and carries a load of 600,000 pounds.

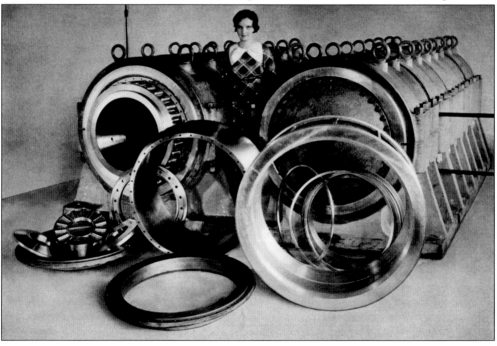

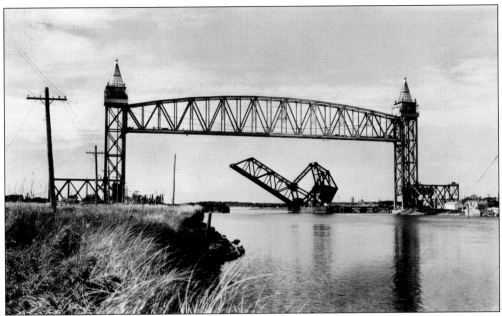

These photographs show the completed railroad bridge shortly before the demolition of the 1911 railroad bridge (above) and several years later, on June 23, 1938 (below). The 1935 railroad bridge is a vertical lift bridge. From its completion until 1959, it held the record for the longest lift span in the world. The high bridges completed for the highways would not have been practical for railroads, as they would have necessitated miles of inclined approach grades. The prominent architectural firm of Mead and White consulted on the obelisk design of the towers, but the engineering was the work of Parsons, Klapp, Brinckerhoff and Douglas, the firm founded by William Barclay Parsons.

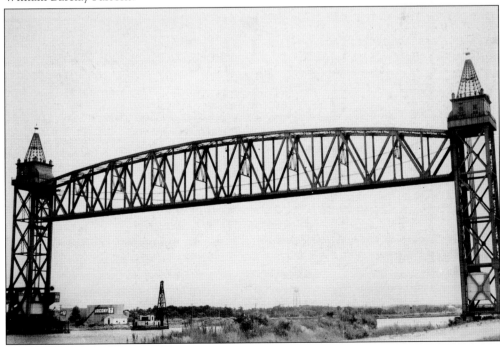

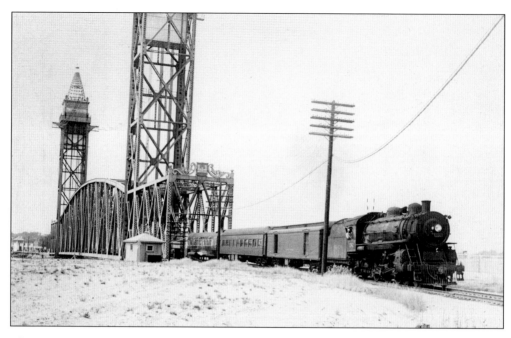

These undated photographs show the bridge in use, with a train exiting the bridge (above). Clearance below the bridge is 7 feet (when lowered) or 135 feet (when raised). Below, men (possibly construction workers) gather at the base of the 1911 bridge, with the new bridge as a backdrop, for a portrait and a toast to "the end of a perfect day."

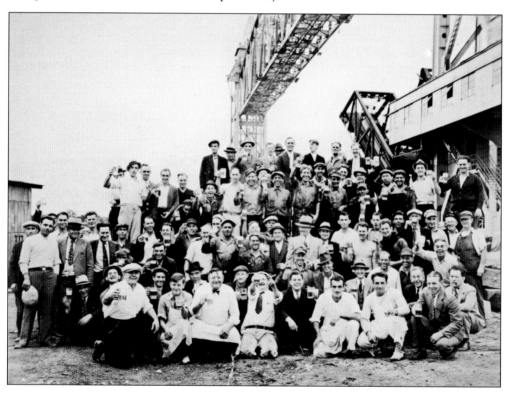

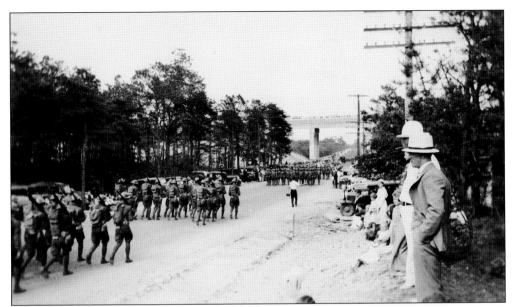

On June 22, 1935, a day of festivities honored the new Cape Cod Canal bridges, including an immense parade with 8,000 participants and a route that stretched over seven miles. More than 100,000 people witnessed the parade, which began at Trading Post Corners and proceeded over the Bourne Bridge. Gov. James Michael Curley cut the ribbon at the Bourne Bridge, while Eleanor R. Belmont, the widow of August Perry Belmont, cut the ribbon at Sagamore Bridge.

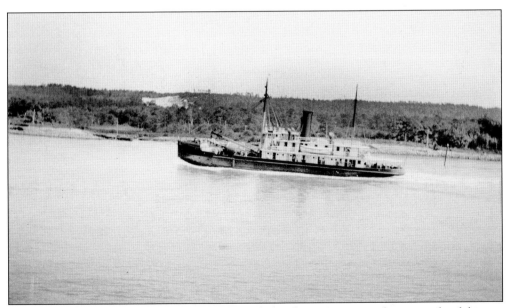

On August 15, 1935, the US Coast Guard lightship *Arbutus* participated in a parade of ships to honor the opening of the bridges.

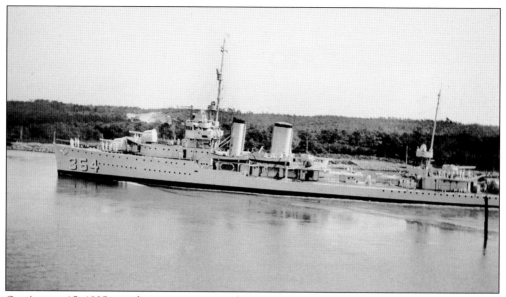

On August 15, 1935, another participant in that parade of ships honoring the canal bridges was the USS *Monaghan*. The last of the Farragut-class destroyers, the *Monaghan* launched from the Boston Navy Yard in 1935. On December 7, 1941, it rammed and sank a Japanese midget sub at Pearl Harbor, Hawaii, during the Japanese air attack. The *Monaghan* served valiantly in the Battle of Midway and at Saipan, Guam, and the Aleutians before being lost in a typhoon in 1944.

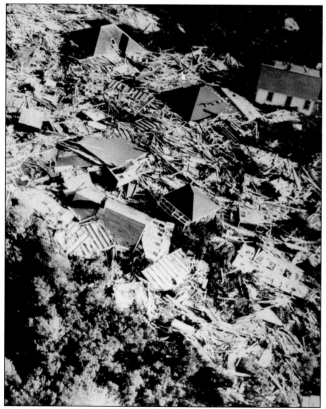

Houses were smashed and overturned all along Buzzards Bay after the New England Hurricane of September 21, 1938. Over 700 people were killed in the surprise storm, mostly on Long Island and along the southern coast of New England. (Photograph by the Weather Bureau, US Department of Commerce.)

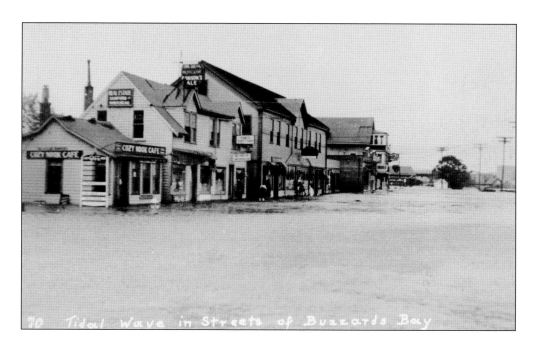

In the aftermath of the New England Hurricane of 1938, floodwaters surged into the business district in Bourne (above) and completely submerged cars at the depot in Buzzards Bay (below). Historically, storm surges have traveled up Buzzards Bay into Bourne at irregular intervals, but with great intensity. The Great Colonial Hurricane in 1635 destroyed the Aptucxet Trading Post, while an 1869 storm surge flooded Bourne, washed out the railroad bridge at Buzzards Bay station, and deposited boats far inland.

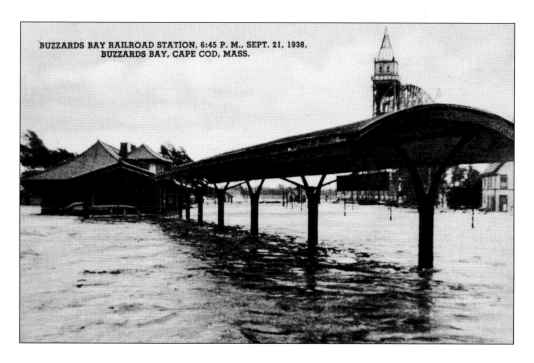

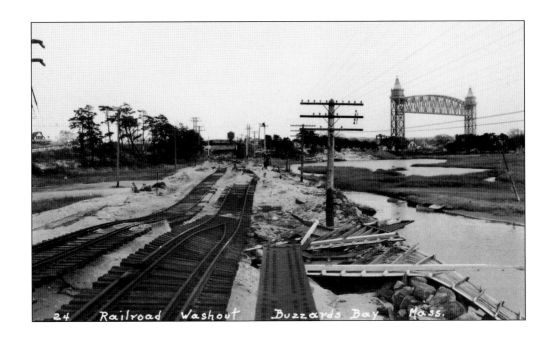

The New England Hurricane of 1938 washed out long stretches of railroad track in Buzzards Bay (above) and piled up buildings along the shoreline in Bourne (below). The storm destroyed 9,000 buildings, 26,000 automobiles, 3,000 boats, and damaged countless more.

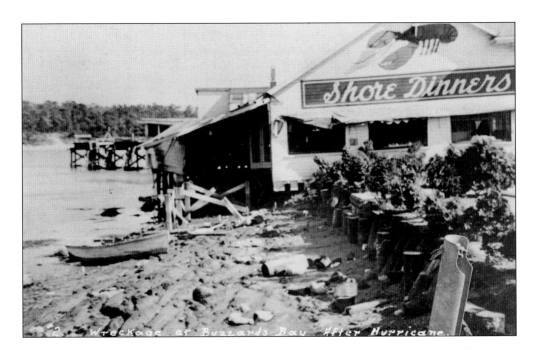

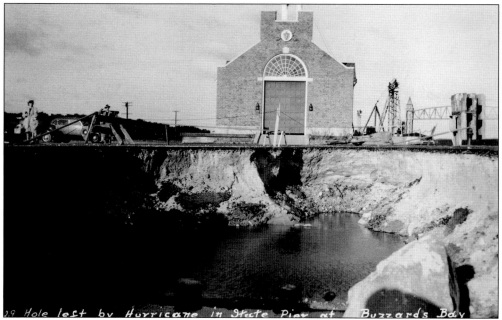

The New England Hurricane of 1938 gouged a huge hole in Commonwealth Pier in Bourne, barely sparing the new (1932) Commonwealth Pier Building. Designed by the Boston architectural firm of Read, Everett, and Clements, the building anchored a new government complex on Taylor's Point at the southwest entrance to the canal.

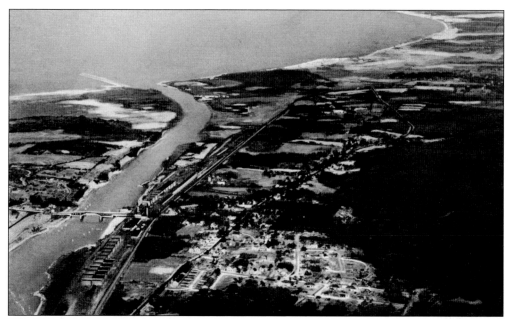

This aerial photograph shows the Cape Cod Bay end of the canal from the air in the 1930s, before completion of the Sagamore Bridge in 1935. Photographer Howard M. Wood had a studio in New Bedford and took many aerial photographs of Cape Cod in the 1920s and 1930s. (Photograph by Howard M. Wood; courtesy of the William Brewster Nickerson Archives.)

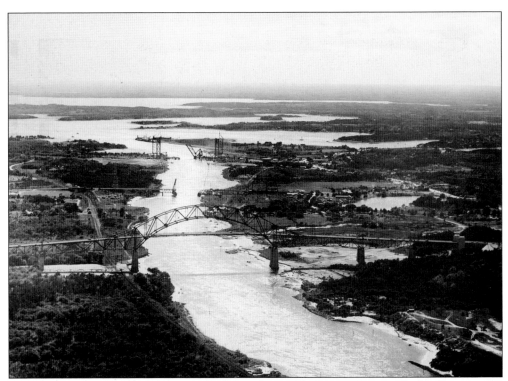

At the Buzzards Bay end of the Cape Cod Canal in 1935, the new Bourne Bridge (foreground) is open, but the vertical span of the Buzzards Bay Railroad Bridge has not been completed yet. Between them, the old Bourne Bridge has been partially dismantled. (Photograph by Howard M. Wood; courtesy of the William Brewster Nickerson Archives.)

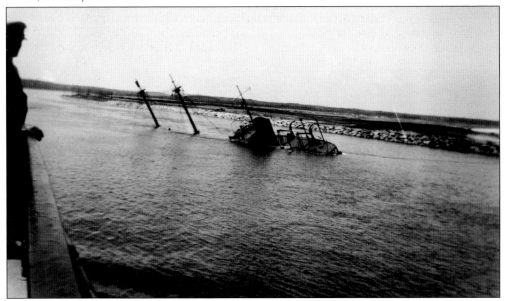

On May 5, 1951, the *Arizona Sword* crashed into the *Berwindvale* just east of the Sagamore Bridge and sank. It took a year to unload its cargo of sulphur and refloat it. Though infrequent, wrecks continue to happen in the Cape Cod Canal.

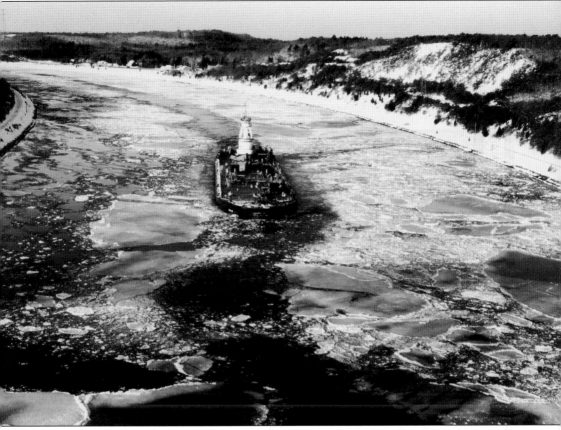

Winter conditions complicate travel through the Cape Cod Canal in this 1986 photograph. Although the tides may sometimes cause treacherous currents in the Cape Cod Canal, the persistent argument against introducing a lock has been that the tides prevent the canal from freezing over. As it approaches its centennial, the Cape Cod Canal has a rich past and a limitless future. (Photograph by the US Army Corps of Engineers.)

BIBLIOGRAPHY

Anti-Friction Bearing Design for Movable Span Bridges. South Bend, IN: Torrington Company, 1950.

Cape Cod Ship Canal Company: Charter and Its Amendments, Contracts for Construction, Supreme Court Decisions, etc. Boston: Rockwell and Churchill, 1887.

Carradine, Reed. "The New Canal and Old Cape Cod." *Harper's Weekly.* January 11, 1908: 16–17.

"The Conquest of Cape Cod." *Harper's Weekly.* July 17, 1909: 13.

Conway, J. North. *The Cape Cod Canal: Breaking Through the Bared and Bended Arm.* Charleston SC: The History Press, 2008.

Dalton, J.W. *The Cape Cod Canal Illustrated.* Sandwich, MA: J.W. Dalton, 1911.

Farson, Robert H. *The Cape Cod Canal.* 1977. 2nd ed. Yarmouth Port, MA: Cape Cod Historical Publications, 1987.

Keene, Betsy D. *History of Bourne from 1622 to 1937.* 1937. Rpt. Bourne, MA: Bourne Historical Society, 1975.

Kimball, Edwin Fiske. "On the Shores of Buzzards Bay." *New England Magazine.* September 1892: 3–25.

A Little Visit to the Cape Cod Canal: Selected Views Showing the New Inland Waterway in the Making. Buzzards Bay, MA: Cape Cod Camera Craft, 1913.

Massachusetts Historical Commission. *MHC Reconnaissance Report: Bourne.* 1984.

Quinn, William P. *Shipwrecks Around Cape Cod (Illustrated).* Farmington, ME: Knowlton & McLeary, 1973.

Reid, William James. *The Building of the Cape Cod Canal 1627–1914.* PhD diss., Boston University, 1958. Privately printed, 1961.

Report of the Joint Committee of 1860 upon the Proposed Canal to Unite Barnstable and Buzzard's Bays. Boston, MA: Wright & Potter, 1864.

Vuilleumier, Marion R. *Images of America: Sagamore Beach.* Charleston, SC: Arcadia Publishing, 2003.

ABOUT
HISTORIC NEW ENGLAND

Historic New England is the oldest, largest, and most comprehensive regional heritage organization in the nation. With its 36 properties spanning five states, it brings history to life while preserving the past for everyone interested in exploring the authentic New England experience from the 17th century to today. The organization shares the region's history through vast collections, publications, public programs, museum properties, archives, and family stories documenting more than 400 years of life in New England. For more information, visit HistoricNewEngland.org.

Discover Thousands of Local History Books Featuring Millions of Vintage Images

Arcadia Publishing, the leading local history publisher in the United States, is committed to making history accessible and meaningful through publishing books that celebrate and preserve the heritage of America's people and places.

Find more books like this at
www.arcadiapublishing.com

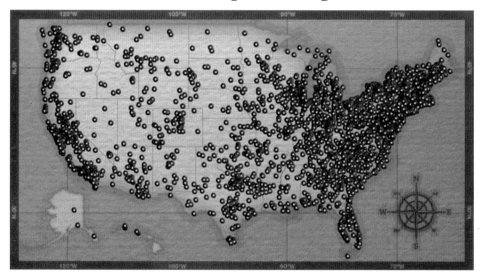

Search for your hometown history, your old stomping grounds, and even your favorite sports team.

Consistent with our mission to preserve history on a local level, this book was printed in South Carolina on American-made paper and manufactured entirely in the United States. Products carrying the accredited Forest Stewardship Council (FSC) label are printed on 100 percent FSC-certified paper.

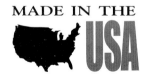

MADE IN THE USA